REACHING THE PERISHING

A Country Preacher's Life Story

Dr. Johnny Woodard ~ DD

First Printing - 2009
Second Printing – 2015
Third Printing – 2016

Published by Revival Waves of Glory Books & Publishing
PO Box 596| Litchfield, Illinois 62056 USA
www.revivalwavesofgloryministries.com

Revival Waves of Glory Books & Publishing is committed to excellence in the publishing industry.

Book design Copyright © 2015 by Revival Waves of Glory Books & Publishing.
All rights reserved.
Library of Congress Control Number: 2016933688
(Revival Waves of Glory), Revival Waves of Glory, Litchfield, IL.

EBook: 978-3-9602-8384-3
Paperback: 978-0692642306
Hardcover: 978-1-60796-960-0

Published in the United States of America

Table of Contents

Introduction

In August of 1995, Dr. Jack Meeks, Bro. Jack Parker and myself stood on the terrace of the King David Hotel in Tel Avi, Israel and watched the sun sink below the horizon in the Mediterranean Sea. I videoed the sun as it rapidly disappeared out of sight and was amazed at how fast it vanished from sight.

It made me realize more than ever the importance of the scripture in God's word that tells us to redeem the time for the present days are evil. Jesus' first recorded words were, "*And he said unto them, how is it that ye sought me? Wist ye not that I must be about my Father's business?*" His last recorded words before dying were "It is finished." I am so thankful that God extended His hand of mercy to me and saved my soul when I was a young boy. No greater sacrifice has ever been made than when God gave His only begotten Son as an atonement for the sins of the whole world.

This book tells the story of how God worked in my life, from the time I was born to a poor family living in a small community named Morgan's Bluff, just north of Orange, Texas on the Sabine River, to the present. He sent many special people in my life, as He prepared me for the world-wide ministry that I am involved in today. Who would have ever thought that a simple country preacher would someday preach to billions on worldwide radio and be president of a Bible Correspondence Institute with students around the world?

One of the most popular Gospel hymns of the day is "Amazing Grace." The same grace that saves us also keeps us and guides and directs us into all truth. To God be the glory for how He has worked in my life and the lives of those He put in my path, to help fulfill His great plan for the ages. As the sun sets on our lives, let us not be weary in well doing!

Dedication

This book is dedicated to my wife, Jewel. Her countless years of hard work grading tests, printing and assembling courses, preparing mail, printing, cutting and folding tracts, as well as being faithful to God in her walk with Him, is a great part of where this ministry is today.

Without her help, prayers and encouragement, The Bread Of Life International Bible Correspondence Institute would not be the success it is today. She is truly a "Jewel" in every aspect of her commitment to God.

Johnny & Jewel Woodard

The Bread Of Life International
Bible Correspondence Institute
P.O. Box 334
Kirbyville, Texas 75956

bolbcs@gmail.com

http://freebibleschool.simplesite.com/

Special Thanks
&
Recognition

My heartfelt gratitude to those who devoted their time and talents to help make this book a reality.

Proofreading & words of encouragement
Annette Carranza
Jewel Woodard
Jan Rusk
Janis Davis
Bro. Paul Skinner
Joshua Woodard

Foreword

I first met Brother Johnny Woodard and family while preaching a revival meeting at First Baptist Church of Evadale, Texas. He and his daughters sang some Blue Grass Gospel. From the first meeting, I knew he wanted to count for our Lord Jesus. He began serving the Lord in pastoral work and was a pastor to several churches while learning and acquiring Bible knowledge while seeking to follow the perfect will of God. He visited Mexico several times, having a burden for missions and wanting to really count for the Lord with his life.

As he matured in the faith and knowledge of God's Word, he became more and more interested in mission outreach and eventually surrendered to do full time mission work, via radio, correspondence school and distribution of all kinds of Christian literature, including Bibles and lessons he designed for his students and all who wanted to use them for outreach. Also, he authored several Christian tracts for general use worldwide. With the Lord blessing and guiding him, he and his precious wife Jewel have established a great outreach to the world.

I can truly say, Brother Johnny and Sister Jewel are real, and that says a lot, for there are so many charlatans in the world today. It surely is great to know some real sure enough Christian Servants. My wife Olene and I count it a great honor of our Heavenly Father in allowing us to have them as fellow missionaries and close friends.

Bro. Cliff Brown
Field Director
The Bread Of Life Baptist Missionary Fellowship, Combes, Texas

We have known Bro. Johnny Woodard for thirty some-odd years, as pastor, preacher, teacher, evangelist, musician and friend. His ministry is one of the many miracles that we have witnessed as we serve in the Lord's work together.

The sacrifices that he and his family have made are great, and we know that he will continue to be blessed by God for his obedience. We are proud to call him our friend and brother in Christ.

Bro. David & Sis. Jackie Richmond
Grace Baptist Church
Evans, Louisiana

Bro. David & Sis. Jackie Richmond

Dr. Johnny Woodard, a man, chosen of God, not of men. He is our John The Baptist of this time. In the Kingdom Of God, God has always had His specialists, whose chief concern has been the moral breakdown, the decline in the Spiritual health of the nation or the church.

Such men were Elijah, Jeremiah, Paul, Johnny Woodard and others of their kind, who appeared at critical times in history to reprove, rebuke and exhort in the name of God and for righteousness. We love you Johnny, keep up the good work.

Dr. Jack Meeks
Founder:
The Bread Of Life Victory Hour
And
The Bread Of Life International
Bible Correspondence Institute

Dr. Jack Meeks

The Woodard Boys
Top
J.E - Roy - Huebert
Bottom
Darrell - R.L. - Johnny

Daddy & "Ma"

Chapter I
Early Childhood

I was the youngest of seven boys and was born on December 24, 1946, in a small community located on the Sabine River between Orange and Deweyville, Texas. The oldest to the youngest brothers' names are J.E., R.L., Huebert Avis, Roy Lee, Darrell Wayne and myself, Johnny Ray Woodard. The two oldest brothers were named after my parents by giving them their initials. J.E. stands for James Edwin and R.L. stands for Ruby Lovis. The first-born brother was not named, as he died during childbirth. The little community had only a very small number of families living there, but there were quite a few people from different towns in Southeast Texas that had camp houses. I was not aware that the first born in my family had died at childbirth until my early elementary school years and it really broke my heart. I cried and cried because I truly believed that I would never see my brother because I had no Bible teaching concerning the afterlife. It was only until I was saved a few years later that great joy filled my heart when I understood that he was already waiting for me in Heaven.

The house we lived in had three rooms. There was a kitchen and living room with a big double bed in it, where mama and daddy slept. All six boys slept in a room across the back. It had about a four-inch step down to it. I remember during the big flood in 1953 that water got high enough to get into the bedroom, but not quite in the living room. There was no such thing as evacuation, we lived in the house and waded water to bed. The old house had no insulation, and you could literally see daylight through the cracks in the wall. We had a wood heater in the middle of the living room. You could stand by it and toast on the front side and freeze on the backside. Many times, one of us would grab one's pant leg and pull it against the calf of their leg and nearly blister them. We had no inside bathroom. When it was warm enough, we would all take a bath in the river. During cold weather, we would all have to take a sponge bath.

My next to the oldest brother enlisted in the army about the time I started school and was sent to Germany. He sent a portion of his monthly check home, and we were able to build a house with four bedrooms and an inside bathroom. We were able to get a butane heater for the living room. The eight-grate butane heater kept the living room and kitchen warm, but the bedrooms were another story. We did not have electric blankets back then. We slept under a blanket and quilts. I remember crawling into those beds and it was like climbing between two slabs of ice. There were times when it was so cold that the only thing I would take off was my shoes. I'd jump in bed, coat and all, and put my head under the cover and shiver and shake until I finally warmed up. One night, one of my brothers went to sleep with the window at the head of his bed raised about four inches. A blue norther blew in that night, and when he woke up the next morning, part of his pillow was coated with ice.

The earliest memories I have of my childhood were when I was about three years old. I remember one of my brothers rolling an old tire down a hill near our old home place. We were poor in those days and having store bought toys were out of the question. I remember spending many days rolling an old lawn mower wheel down the road with a flattened out Prince Albert tobacco can that was nailed to the end of a stick. We would spend hours and hours rolling an old tire back and forth to each other in the old dusty road that ran in front of the house. I remember one incident when one of my brothers curled himself up inside a big grader tire, and another one of my brothers rolled him down the road. Needless to say, when he got out of the tire his head was spinning.

We lived so close to the Sabine River that you could literally throw a rock across the road into it. We spent a lot of time either in the river, on the river or by the river. I remember a huge cypress tree on the opposite side of the river, which was the Louisiana side. We would cut a limb about the diameter of one's finger and about four feet long and use it to sling wads of mud across the river. We would get a chunk of the clay that lined the riverbank and crimp it on the end of the limb. We literally spent hours and hours slinging that mud across the river. Of course, we kept tabs on who could throw the most pieces of mud over the top of that big tree on the other side.

Another "sport" of ours during the summer was to walk a mile or so up the river and find a dead tree log that we could roll off into the river and ride it downstream to the house place. Naturally, we would play "King Of The Log", instead of "King Of The Hill." We got quite a few scrapes while being ejected from the soon to be crowned, "King Of The Log," but no serious injuries ever occurred. Sometimes we would also go quite a bit further up the river and bring our "inner tubes" to ride down the river in the sometimes fast, sometimes slow current. Many happy hours were spent on the river. Today people pay a lot of money to ride inner tubes, canoes or rafts down a river or creek. For us, it was an almost everyday affair in the summer months.

Of course, there being six boys living within a few yards of the river, there was a lot of swimming going on. I remember when I was two or three years old, someone gave me a little plastic inner tube that I would put around my waist and go everywhere the big boys went. On many occasions, my brothers or parents would try their best to get me to try to swim without it. It was nothing unusual for me to swim everywhere they went, as long as I had my safety factor with me. I do remember one day they finally convinced me to take it off. I could swim like the rest of them. Our parents were always referred to as "Ma" and "Daddy." I do remember telling "Ma" that she could give that ole inner tube to someone else because I didn't need it anymore. By the time, I was four years old I was a very good swimmer.

Fishing and hunting were also a major part of our lives and livelihood. My father, James E. Woodard, was a commercial fisherman, hunter, and trapper. I can always remember several old wooden boats that could be rented for $1.00 a day. We also sold bait shrimp. Many people don't know it, but there are huge amounts of freshwater shrimp in the rivers. They can reach up to about three inches in length. They make great fish bait, especially for hand fishing. We would catch them using what we called a "shrimp box." It was a wooden box about three feet long, eight inches high and eighteen inches wide and made of thin boards about one-quarter inch thick and about three or four inches wide, usually from an apple or orange crate. We would make a throat in one end out of heavy-duty screen wire for the shrimp to swim into. We made a lid for the top of it. Once inside, the shrimp couldn't find their way out. We sold thousands and thousands of these bait shrimp to fishermen, who either owned their own camps or came from town to spend a day on the river. One of my dreaded chores was to have to get up early in the morning and run the "shrimp boxes." It consisted of driving a big wooden boat, usually fourteen feet or longer and seldom ever with an outboard motor bigger than a five horsepower up and down the river. The boxes were first sunk to the bottom by putting an old piece of scrap metal in it. After the wood became "waterlogged", they would sink on their own. They were usually attached to a limb or tree in the river with a piece of old electrical cable that would not rot in the water. The boxes were baited with a slab of Cottonseed Cake, which was a type of animal feed that came in long slabs about three feet long, one inch thick and eighteen inches wide.

Of course, there are many fish tales to tell, along with hunting, trapping, and boat racing. During Spring and Summer, we would sell catfish, shrimp and also rent boats. The catfish were sold live for $.50 a pound and were cleaned free. There was an old fish cleaning board mounted next to the riverbank. A big hook was used to hang the fish on, and they were skinned, not filleted. Daddy and "Ma" skinned and cleaned many a pound of catfish in their days! They were masters at it.

I remember getting up before school and running a few "trotlines" to catch some blue or channel catfish to sell and make spending money. On one occasion Daddy had a line stretched across the river and told me that if I would bait it, I could have all the fish I caught on it. The line was tied to a small willow limb on the Texas side that was very flexible. When I eased the boat up to the line one morning, the limb was as still as a mouse. I figured nothing was on it. As I got a few yards toward the middle of the river, the line suddenly took off so hard and fast that it was all I could do to keep the hooks from hooking me, as I fed the line through my hands. The fish went all the way to the bottom. I began to work my way to the fish again. A few feet from the boat, the catfish came to the surface, and he looked huge to me. I had a big dip net in the boat and tried to dip him up tail first. Bad idea! I found out that the catfish didn't take too well to a dip net being slid over his tail. Every time I would try to dip him up, he would take off again and run until he hit the bottom of the river. After about the third or fourth time of him nearly jerking the line out of my hands, I put the dip net in front of him, and he literally swam into it. If there were any more fish on that trotline, I have no idea. I took the hook out of that catfish's mouth and away I went to the boat dock.

When I got home, we had an old pair of scales, and we weighed him (or her), and the fish weighed a whopping twenty pounds! That was a big fish for a kid in elementary school for sure. A barber that owned a camp house a little way up the road from me gave me $.50 a pound for my fish, and I didn't even have to clean him. I was given a $10.00 bill. I was rich!!!

I baited the hooks with P&G soap. That's right, soap is one of the best catfish baits ever, even to this day. What happened is the twenty-pounder swallowed a small catfish. I remember seeing a picture in the Orange Leader Newspaper around that time of a sixty-pound plus catfish that had been swallowed up to the two big fins behind his gills. The way to know if a catfish had been swallowed on by a bigger fish is that the fish would have white skin and a few scratch marks where the big fish tried to swallow him.

There were some huge catfish in the river. One morning Daddy came and got me up and told me to come outside; he had something to show me. There was a flathead catfish, like the one I caught, hanging on the side of the house that was bigger than me. The fish weighed over ninety pounds! My oldest brother has caught a lot of big catfish himself, the biggest being over seventy pounds. The big catfish were usually caught on live bait. The best big catfish baits back then were a yellow cat (pollywog), a carp, bream or small channel cat.

I remember going with daddy to seine some bait out of a drain ditch that crossed a road. There was a culvert running under the road, and nearly all of the fish were in that small concrete culvert pipe. Daddy had me to take a garden hoe and crawl through the culvert. It was literally working alive with small fish, perch, carp, etc. I pushed the hoe ahead of me, along with the fish (and a water moccasin or two) out the other end into a waiting net, where Daddy scooped them up and put them in a 5-gallon bucket of water to keep them alive. We seined a lot of baitfish to keep all the many trotlines baited. We seined perch, little grinnell (cypress bass), pollywogs and crawfish for live bait, when not fishing with soap.

My daddy was probably the greatest hunter around in his day and time. It was not unusual to kill between 50 and 100 cat squirrels in a single day. We ate our share of them, but most were sold to "City Folks" who didn't hunt. I remember going squirrel hunting with daddy once. While we were walking through the woods, me behind him, he whispered, "Stop, there's a squirrel." I looked and looked and finally said: "where?" "In that big tree just ahead," he said. I looked and looked and he was finally able to get me focused on a tree ahead that looked about ¼ mile off. I finally saw a cat squirrel on a limb. The squirrel was so far away that he looked about 2 or 3 inches long. It would have taken an elephant gun to reach the poor critter from that far. We were able to get close enough for him to get a shot at him with his old 12-gauge pump shotgun. The gun was a true antique; it had a hammer on it. It was quite an impressive gun and is worth a lot of money today.

I remember Daddy getting a 10-gauge double barrel shotgun with hammers on it. It had quite a kick to it, to say the least. One of my brothers, Roy, took a liking to the gun and would take it squirrel hunting with him. He said no matter how hard he tried, he could not keep the gun from rising up and his thumb hitting him in the nose every time he shot it. It was quite an impressive weapon for sure. I am not sure what ever happened to it. I do remember that Daddy had it in a gun rack in his bedroom. One day while working on the bathroom, which was adjacent to his bedroom, he was doing some hammering. We heard a terrible noise. It sounded like either a stick of dynamite, a sonic boom or an atomic bomb had gone off in his bedroom. Upon going into his room, we saw that the ten gauge had fallen out of the gun rack and hit the floor. Naturally, it hit with both hammers and both barrels went off at the same time. It blew a hole through the dividing wall into the next bedroom and right through the next bedroom wall and exited outside. I am not sure, but those hammers might have had a part in it's departure.

Daddy was also an excellent trapper. He trapped during the winter months. Back then mink were very valuable. He could get up to $30.00 for a big mink hide. I have helped him skin many a raccoon, mink, otter, and possum for the pelts. There is a special technique to skinning an animal in order to preserve its hide. After skinning a mink, otter or possum, the skin was stretched over a board, with the fur on the inside. The skin was then left out in the sun to dry. Raccoons were skinned, so their pelts would be in a square configuration. They were then stretched out and nailed to a piece of plywood, with the fur inside. When they dried, they could be kept until the fur buyer came. I have watched Daddy set his steel traps and cover them with wet leaves where different animals were sure to travel. I felt sorry for the trapped animals. I never really got into hunting. When I was hunting, it was not for sport, it was for food. I have always liked most any kind of wild game. We had a diet of squirrels, rabbits, hogs and fish. We even made our own cracklings and hog lard from fat hogs that ran wild in the woods. I wonder how much cholesterol was in that homemade hog lard?

My mother was a very talented woman. She was one of the best seamstresses around. She could look at a picture of the most fancy dress, or most any piece of clothing, make her own patterns and sew it together like a regular store-bought garment. She had a great talent for making all kinds of cloth dolls. She would sew them together, stuff them with cotton, and use yarn for their hair. She would stitch their eyes, nose, and mouth with different colored embroidery thread. She sold many dolls to people who were friends or work acquaintances. In all the days I remember of my Daddy being self-employed and mama selling dolls, dresses, shirts, caps, etc., there was never an ad put anywhere, nor was there a poster put up. Everything was advertised by word of mouth.

Mama was a hard working lady who did everything she could to make the best of what we had to do with. She would make shirts out of 25-pound flour sacks. She would patch our clothes, as long as it was needed, in order to get all the use out of them we could. She washed many a load of clothes on a rub board before she got her first ringer type-washing machine. Of course, the clothes were hung up on a clothesline to dry in the sunshine. I remember well her using an old iron to iron clothes with. It was placed on the old wood heater to get it hot enough to get the wrinkles out of the clothes. She would take an old glass coke bottle, fill it with water, and then put a bunch of straws in the mouth to sprinkle water on the clothes she was ironing. For a long time, we had an old hand water pump that we had to pump water from for house use. Sometimes we would have to "prime the pump" before we could get water from it. She pumped many a gallon of water for sure.

"Ma" was also a great cook. I never remember her having a recipe. She would bake big cathead biscuits three times a day. During hard times, we could not afford to keep the fish or game. We had many a meal of biscuits, fried potatoes, and gravy. Now Sunday was different; we would have a big pot of navy beans, cornbread, and a homemade cake. Times were not always that bad. I do remember some great meals of fresh pork ribs, wood ducks, squirrels, rabbits, deer, fish or an occasional raccoon. I can remember trying armadillo once, but I can't recall what it tastes like. In some of my mission travels, I have eaten a lot worse than that for sure.

I can remember at times that big blue crabs would come up the river from Sabine Lake, and we would catch them and "Ma" would make a big pot of crab gumbo. She made her own roux, and I cannot ever remember eating any better. Back then no one had heard of BBQ Crabs, which is a sensation here now. Sometimes we would boil the crabs and eat them and the big pinchers. They were delicious for sure. My mother could not eat shrimp. She ate them one time and almost died from an allergic reaction. A lot of people don't know it, but one of the best ways to eat crabs is to clean them and fry the body in cornmeal, like fish.

Me being the youngest of seven children, I did not see as many hard times as my older brothers did. My parents had moved to Orange from Sabine County near San Augustine, Texas before I was born. To the best of my knowledge, I was the only one of seven children that were delivered by a real doctor. Midwives delivered my other brothers and, no doubt, it was a very painful experience for my mother. I seldom went to a doctor for anything as a child. I fell off a fence gate one time and snapped my right arm between the wrist and elbow. My hand was about eight inches from where it should have been. My arm was laid on a table and "set" and a splint put on it. No pain medication, no shots, no doctor visits, no X-Rays. I was almost twenty years old before I took any store-bought pain medication.

"Ma" knew the old home remedies. I well remember taking a big tablespoon of sugar with kerosene on it for the "croup." She knew how to make a poultice that could draw the infection out of a wound. The only times I remember going to the doctor as a child is on two occasions. The first time, one of my feet got badly infected from scratching it because of "athlete's foot." That is one time that the poultice didn't work. I had several red streaks going up my foot and already starting up my leg. A trip to the doctor and some antibiotics did the job. The other occasion like to have done me in. The Barber neighbor had a big cornfield, and it sure had some nice roasting ears in it. I snuck into it and plucked me thirteen ears of corn. I carried them down to the riverbank so no one could see me and ate all thirteen ears, RAW!! Later that day, Maw couldn't understand why my stomach was cramping, and I was dry heaving until I couldn't dry heave anymore. A trip to the doctor took care of it. Believe it or not, it has been only a few short years ago, (I am sixty nine now) that I could even stand the smell of corn on the cob, let alone eat it!

My mama and daddy had a hard life. They were not active in church when I was at home. My mother said she attended church faithfully when she was first married, but quit going. I have the assurance in my heart that I will see them in Heaven again someday. In their older years, they both assured me that they had asked Jesus to come into their heart, and they both had the assurance of salvation. Both of them had the opportunity to hear me preach and my family sing. What a comfort it is to know that salvation is not based on feelings, church membership, baptism or good works. Salvation takes place in the heart when one puts their trust in the finished work of Jesus on Calvary's cross.

I don't see how I could leave out a vital part of my early childhood days on the Sabine River without writing about boat racing. As I stated before, I learned to swim at four years of age. I was also an accomplished boat racer at not much older than that. My oldest brother had a homemade wooden boat about twelve or thirteen feet long. He brought a brand new twelve-horse Sea King outboard motor and put on it. It would scat across the water pretty good. I remember being far too little to crank the motor and my brother cranking it for me. He would then take the boat paddle out of the boat and push the boat away from the dock and say, "take off." Take off I would. I would give the gas to that motor; it would jump up on top of the water and away we would go. I would run that boat wide open up and down the river in front of the house while my family, people from the camps and anyone else who happened to drive up would be lined up and down the bank watching me rip and tear up and down the river until they would flag me in. A boat racing accident would play a major role in my rededicating my life to Jesus when I was twenty-nine years old and thrown from a fast boat. By God's grace, I was spared from harm or death. I will give the details in a later chapter. There will be some more of our fast boat stories in a later chapter.

There are many people who do not believe that a young child can be saved. I would refer them to the Bible, when Jesus rebuked His disciples and outright commanded them to bring little children to Him, for of such is the Kingdom of Heaven. I was saved in March of 1954 at Little Cypress Baptist Church, just outside Orange, Texas. I was just over seven years old. I will never forget that morning as long as I live unless I lose my senses. There was a very special lady that God put in our family's lives. A couple named Sam and Aileen Trussel lived about three-quarters of a mile up the road from us. She was a faithful member of the Little Cypress Baptist Church. I remember her coming and picking me up and bringing me to Sunday School and church faithfully. Another special person that God put into my life was Bro. Wilburn Ansley, pastor of the church. I cannot remember the messages he preached. I do remember that in one message he mentioned people buying electric clothes dryers. He said he wanted God's sunshine to dry his clothes. He was a dynamic preacher of God's word and has been used of God for many years. I do remember the Sunday morning coming down the aisle during the invitation time. I was under great conviction with tears streaming down my face. I will never forget the question he asked me when he met me at the front. He didn't ask me if I wanted to join the church, he didn't ask me if I wanted to get baptized, he didn't even ask me if I wanted to get saved. His simple words were "Son, what do you need." My reply was "I need to be saved." His reply was simple, "Do you believe Jesus died for you?" There were no laying on of hands or praying at the altar, I simply put my trust in Jesus that morning, and I have never been the same since.

CHAPTER II
My Teenage Years

I was able to live on the Sabine River until 1965, the year I graduated High School at Little Cypress. When I started school there in the first grade and graduated, the entire school was in one location. I remember when I was in the sixth grade we were in a classroom that was half sixth graders and half-seventh graders. There were no changing classes back then. The teacher, Mr. Beltz, would teach us for a while and then switch over to teaching the seventh graders. I was his favorite student and was on the honor roll for the fifth, sixth and seventh grades. I remember taking school pictures in an old pair of blue jeans that had a huge patch over one of the knees. I tried my best to hide that patch with my hand, but it stuck out like a sore thumb. It was not uncommon for kids to go to school barefooted in those days, but to the best of my knowledge, I always had a pair of shoes to cover my feet.

One thing I remember most about my teenage years was having a couple of motor scooters. They were a lot different than the motorbikes of today. They had a 5 HP Motor that you had to kick start on the front of the motor. The kick-starter operated on gears. You would have to raise it up with your foot and then kick it down. I limped around many a day with a sore foot when the gear would not engage, and you would slam your foot against the floor with all your weight on it. They had a centrifugal clutch that engaged when you gave the motor the gas. I remember on one occasion that the pads in the clutch of an old scooter wore out, and I did not have the two or three dollars to buy a new set. What does one do in such a case? Well, parking my only source of transportation was out of the question, so I improvised. I drilled holes on the hub assembly that the clutches engaged to and put bolts in it. That made it a direct drive. It ran great! The only inconvenience was getting going. I would have to push the motor scooter, with the motor turning over, and when it fired, jump on the seat before it ran off and left me. Like I said, it ran as fast as ever. The only problem was getting started and stopping. When stopping, the slower you got, the more the scooter lurched every time the motor fired. But as the old saying goes, "You gotta do what you gotta do."

I rode my motor scooter all over. It was licensed and street legal. They did not require an inspection sticker back then. One of the most fun things to do was to put straight pipes on the exhaust. I found out that an old thin walled metal vacuum cleaner pipe really sounded off. They produced a deep mellow sound, and when you got up some speed, you could let off on the gas and listen to that pipe pop like a miniature bomb. If you really wanted it to "rack off", you could find an old car horn and cut the end of it off and attach it to the end of the pipe. I remember the first time I rode my motor scooter to school. Naturally, there had to be an inspection crew to go over it for you and give their opinion. Their opinions always varied and were always given whether you wanted them or not. One of the inspectors, upon seeing the horn protruding from the back of my cool ride asked me a question I have never forgotten. He said, "What is the funnel for, to put oil in it as fast as it burns it? As you can imagine, he was not my best friend, EVER!!!

Another fun thing about riding those scooters was the fact that the lights ran off a magneto. What that means is that the faster you ran the scooter, the brighter the lights got. I remember one of my older brothers going to a Frankenstein movie in Orange, which was about ten or twelve miles from home. It was late at night, and there was a right-hand turn he had to make to get on the road that would take him to the house in about two miles. He knew if he slowed that scooter down to make that turn, his headlight would get so dim he would not be able to see what was lurking in the woods. So, he decided he could make that ninety-degree right hand turn fast enough to keep that light, bright enough to scare all the monsters off that were sure to get him if he slowed down. Well, that plan didn't go exactly as he thought. He found himself and the scooter in the ditch, and it was pitch dark. My brother has never been a big person, even now. But to this day, he or none of the rest of us knows how he was able to get that motor scooter out of that ditch and on the road, with that headlight glaring, before Frankenstein could even get close to him, let alone claim him as a victim. Those old Cushman scooters would run about 60 mph when they finally got wound up. Not bad for a 5 HP four stroke motor.

I also remember buying a little Go Cart with a 6 HP, two-stroke engine on it. That little Go Cart was so small I could barely get in the seat. But that six horse motor would fly. It would run so fast it would bring tears to your eyes, and you were sitting about four inches above the ground. I remember when the motor finally quit on it. I tried putting an old chainsaw motor on it, but it would barely move the Go Cart. The only logical thing to do was to pull it behind a car. Naturally, a school buddy wanted to be the first to try it out. I still don't know how he survived being pulled on that little Go Cart behind a 54 Chevy Bellaire, so fast he was darting from one side of the road to the other, especially when the driver hit passing gear.

Boats were always a great part of our recreation in those days. My friend who test-drove the Go Cart decided we should build us a boat of our own. We got the lumber and plywood and made a little flat bottom boat about 8 feet long and three feet wide. No matter how many nails we used to nail it together, when we put it in the water it sunk like an anchor. We fished it out and after it had dried out; we figured if Noah could seal a boat as big as the Ark with pitch (Tar), we could surely make our little boat float. We got us a big block of tar and heated it up and painted the bottom of our boat and a little way up each side with that tar. My friend and I were proud of our accomplishment and couldn't wait to try it out. There was one minor problem; my friend had about as much tar on him as that little boat did. As you can imagine, all that tar on him was near to impossible to get off. He came up with the only logical solution, there was. He poured a five-gallon can of gasoline in his bathtub, stripped off, and sat down in the gasoline. As you can imagine, he didn't sit long. That gasoline didn't feel too good on his naked skin, and he came out of that bathtub like he was shot out of a cannon. To this day, I can't remember how he finally got all that tar off him. Whatever happened to our little boat and why that gasoline in the septic system didn't blast his whole house into outer space is a mystery to me.

Another fun event for him and me was to go camping. We went one night, about a half a mile below the old house place on the river. He had a 3 HP Johnson or Evinrude outboard motor that he was very proud of. We loaded one of our old rental boats up and headed downstream after dark. We had our fishing gear, a quilt to sleep on and a nice supply of bait shrimp. We had a frying pan and plenty of grease to fry the fish we knew we would catch. Seeing as I was a seasoned professional boat racer since I was 3 or 4 years old and I knew the river, I was the navigator. I was a little disappointed in his motor because it ran fine at high speed, but wouldn't idle down. I also noticed behind the boat there was a cloud of smoke rising up that would put any mosquito sprayer that ever existed to shame. We arrived safely at our camping spot and unloaded the boat. After we had fished awhile, we discovered that the fish were not biting. We had no alternative but to fry the bait shrimp. We gathered some limbs for a fire. Since there was no lighter pine, dry leaves or pine straw, I told my buddy that I would get a little gas out of the gas can in the boat. I got a small can full, and we piled up enough wood for a nice fire. I put enough of the "gas" on the wood to really get it going fast. I struck a match and threw it on the wood as I jumped back away from the fire to keep from getting singed by the sudden flame that would erupt when that "gas" ignited. Well, to our wonder, the match went out and no fire. After all was said and done, we found out he had filled his little 3 HP motor full of kerosene and added an extra can of oil to make sure it was well lubricated.

To get back to the boat racing that I mentioned in a previous chapter, it was in full swing then. Four of my brothers lived to have one thing and one thing only, the fastest boat. The boats got shorter, and the motors got bigger. They mostly raced 20 HP Mercurys, until one would outrun the other one. Then there were only two things to do; either get a smaller boat or bigger motor. One of my brothers (the one Frankenstein couldn't catch) built a little plywood boat about 11 feet long and four feet wide. He ran a 20 HP Mercury on it, and it was really fast. It was also very tricky, as he found out one day. The boat threw him out and ran around in the river wide open for quite a spell. During the process, he had to dive under the water several times as the boat raced over him. The boat propeller did hit him on one foot and cut off his little toe, before running up on the bank and hitting a big cypress tree. He later bought a factory built 13 foot Canalito racing boat. It had a Super 10 Hurricane Mercury outboard on it. It had a "Quicksilver" racing lower unit on it and stacks, which was an open exhaust coming straight out of one side of the head. You could hear it coming from a mile or so. I was told that at one time that 10 HP Mercury ran about 60 mph.

At that time, I didn't have my own racing boat unless you wanted to race with my 1½ HP Evinrude. I remember 3 of us going camping one evening in a big wooden boat about 16 feet long. At that time, we had a 3 HP Scott Attwater outboard on it. A couple of miles up the river, it forked into three prongs and the water was pretty swift. In fact, when we hit that middle channel, it was a dead heat. The motor could hold it's own, but could not move the boat against the swift current. We all three had to break out the boat paddles and help the little motor for a hundred yards or so to make it's way through the swift water. My, how times have changed. If a bass boat doesn't run at least 70 or 80 mph, it is considered slow.

There was another family that lived a mile or so up the road that had three boys who were also involved in the racing. I also remember the oldest son and his wife were killed in a tragic car accident. The other three brothers were right in the midst of our competition. I remember one of them buying a brand new 22 HP Mercury outboard that he ran on a 14-foot aluminum boat. Most all of the boats ran about the same speed. One of my brothers, Roy, bought a 25 HP Wizard. It had a four-cylinder engine and was much heavier than the smaller two-cylinder Mercurys. One thing about the big Wizard was that it had a handle on it, as all the other motors had and did not require a steering wheel. With two people sitting on the back seat of a narrow, 14-foot aluminum boat, along with the weight of that big motor, it was almost like riding a bucking bull. After that motor ran awhile and got warmed up good, it lost its compression and was very hard to start. I remember my brother cranking on that old motor for nearly half an hour with a pull rope, trying to get it fired up. His back would look like he had been flogged and would be covered with red stripes where the crank, rope came across his back time and time again.

My next to the oldest brother, R.L., was more determined than all of us to be the fastest. When his Mark 25 Mercury could not keep up with the others, he had only one alternative, buy a bigger motor. I remember him buying a 30 HP, four cylinder Mercury and putting it on a 12-foot flat bottom plywood boat. He mounted a steering wheel in it and easily outran the others. However, that 30 horse Mercury wasn't quite fast enough for him. He went and bought a Merc 450, a 45 HP Mercury. He had it on a little wooden runabout boat, and it would run well over 40 m.p.h. I remember him mounting that 45 Mercury on the 13 foot Canalito Racing boat one time. I cannot recall if it was ever clocked, but needless to say, it was FAST!

On one occasion, one of the neighbor's boys had a 7 ½ HP Elgin outboard. I don't know where he came up with the boat, but it was tiny. It was maybe 8 feet long and flat bottomed. That Elgin motor would plane that boat out and scat up and down the river fast for a little boat. In fact, one time it scatted a little too good and threw him out. It happened to be in the wintertime and was freezing cold. One of my brothers jumped into his boat and ran down the river and picked him up. I remember him saying, "Let's get out on the bank and build a fire!" With him being soaked and the wind hitting him, by the time he reached our boat dock, he was shaking like a leaf in a storm.

Those boys were always catching critters and making pets out of them. On one occasion they caught a baby skunk and kept him at their house. The little skunk was not demusked and could still pack a wallop if he felt threatened. I will never forget one of their yard dogs going up to the little skunk and trying to sniff his rear end like dogs do. The little skunk gave him a full dose of his "perfume" full in the dog's face. We all laughed until we nearly cried watching that dog plow the ground up with his nose and foaming at the mouth, trying to get rid of that smell.

On another occasion, their yellow Tom Cat thought he would make friends with the little critter. BIG mistake! When that cat tried to pull the same friendly gesture the dog did, he got a full dose in his face too. We never knew whether that cat went through the fence or over it, but he flat out left the country! They also taught me a neat "trick". Put tape on the bottom of a cat's feet and watch him try to shake that tape off. You can never imagine how fast a cat can shake them paws, trying to shake that tape off. That old yellow cat provided everyone with a lot of good entertainment.

One of the best pets that ever came out of the woods was an otter that they caught as a baby and raised. They named him "Fatso" because that best described him. He was one of the prettiest animals I have ever seen. He was completely tame and was never kept in a cage. He ran loose with the dogs and would go hunting with them. When you came up to their driveway, and "Fatso" saw you coming, he would come running out to meet you and jump up on your leg, wanting to be petted. They kept him for a long time and finally sold him to the Houston Zoo.

I also remember a prank the two older brothers pulled on their little brother. They caught a big cow ant. They are bright orange with black stripes and can be up to ½ or ¾ inches long. They have a huge stinger and can inflict a very painful sting. They are one of the hardest insects to kill that I know of. I remember trying to kill one of them by stomping them in dirt or sand. I have seen those big cow ants keep going time and time again after being repeatedly stomped into the ground. Now back to the prank on little brother. It seems that the two older brothers had gone to the store and bought some assorted goodies. After they returned home, they saw a big cow ant in the yard and caught him. They told little brother to "Open your mouth, close your eyes and stick out your tongue, we have a surprise for you." They had a surprise all right; they dropped that big cow ant on his tongue! I cannot remember how much damage was done, but I do know that little brother learned a valuable lesson, never trust your older brothers again.

Back then there were no fancy toys, and as I stated before, we had to amuse ourselves the best way we could. Those neighborhood boys were masters of using yard animals for entertainment. I remember them taking one of their mama's laying hens in the house. They had an old wood heater like the one we had in earlier years. The inside would be covered with "soot". They would take that chicken

38

and rub him inside the heater while it was not being used and cover that chicken with black soot in several places. They would then take the chicken out in the yard and turn him loose with the rest of the chickens. Naturally, the other chickens thought a stranger had invaded their territory, and they would all jump on that poor chicken. Those boys would laugh until they cried watching those chickens attack the poor victim. I don't recall any serious harm ever coming to anyone from any of their pranks.

On one occasion they took one of their hunting dogs with them on a hunting trip and forgot and left him locked up in the trunk of their car. It was in the middle of summer, and later that evening when they got back to their car, they remembered the dog in the trunk. When they opened the trunk, the poor dog was almost baked and had died a horrible death. It was a terrible accident for sure.

The pranks us boys played back then were considered mischievous but never meant to really harm any of the animals or each other for that matter. Today, pranks result in innocent people being maimed or killed. There was an old man who lived a little way up the road from us who was a victim of a few of our pranks. I remember us pushing his old car down the road to where there was a sandbar and also a red clay bank. My brothers took that wet, red clay and literally covered his old car with it and left it out in the sun to dry. By the time, he found his car, that claywas baked on and it was almost impossible for him to remove it. Of course, they had to have a little "icing on the cake", so they stuffed a potato in his tailpipe!

Christmas time always found us popping firecrackers. That old man was also the object of our attention. We would wait until after dark and then bombard his yard and house with firecrackers. Back then, the firecrackers were much bigger and more powerful than those today. They had cherry bombs and TNT bombs that were very powerful. Those two firecrackers had fuses that could burn underwater. We would cover them with mud, light them and throw them in the river. When they exploded, there would be a huge circle of red light under the water. On several occasions, a fish or two would happen to be swimming by, and they would come floating to the surface.

One night my oldest brother had a huge firecracker "bomb." Way back then, that bomb cost a whole dollar and was huge. It was probably as round as a hardball. My brother decided that he would shoot the big bomb over the old man's house. The bomb was laid down at the proper angle to go over his house, and the fuse was lit. The bomb went off but didn't make it over his house. It landed on his tin roof and went off. It sounded like a major war had broken out. The noise was deafening, to say the least. That old man came out of his house with a 22 rifle, cussing and ranting and raving. I'll never forget his words as he came with his rifle, trying to see us, who were all hiding behind some big trees. "Alright, you d*** Woodard boys, I know you're out there!!"

It would only be right to share some of my experiences with some of my school friends. I had one particular friend who was one of my best friends from elementary school until we graduated. He had an older brother that pulled a few good pranks at school. He has been known to bring chicken snakes to school and turn them loose in the classroom. I also remember that we got involved in building model rockets. You could order a rocket engine from Penrose, Colorado. The engines were about the size of a shotgun shell and when ignited, would put out up to 16 lbs. of thrust. I built a little rocket about 10 or 12 inches high. I put one of the big 16 lb. thrust engines in it. I used a cloth netting to glue the fins onto the bottom of the rocket with airplane glue. I lit the fuse on that little rocket, and it took off so fast, to this day; I have no idea where it went. All I remember is it leaving like a bolt of lightning and those three fins on the little rocket come floating down to the ground. It left so fast it literally tore the fins off the body of the rocket.

The older brother decided that he would make his own rocket fuel and mixed a few items together and brought the powder to school in a jar. During one of the breaks, he poured some of the powder outside at the back of one of the classrooms. That powder sent up a huge cloud of smoke and caught the attention of everyone, including the principal.

I spent many nights with my two friends. The older brother had a newspaper route and had to get up really early to take care of it. To say that he was a heavy sleeper is a huge understatement. When we would go to bed that night, he would place a Big Ben windup alarm clock inside a big pot at the head of his bed. The clock had two ringer bells on top of it and a hammer that would strike those bells when it came time to get up. I remember hearing that clock go off about 4:00 or 4:30 a.m. and it scared me half to death. As for the older brother, he never so much as twitched a muscle.

I went with him one morning to help deliver the newspapers. The papers were folded in squares, and as we drove by, the papers would be thrown on the person's porch, doorsteps or in the yard, where the customer could easily pick them up. That was the plan, and he was an expert at sailing those papers on the front steps, the front porch or neatly in the yard. As for myself, when he let me throw the papers while sitting behind him on the motorcycle, things didn't work out quite as good as his delivery. There were a few calls from angry customers later that morning who had the audacity to complain about their paper being on the roof of their house or maybe in a tree! Anyway, after that, I decided not to pursue a career delivering newspapers.

Another good friend of mine was pretty good at pulling pranks himself. He would love to make our school bus driver mad as possible. I remember the driver had a peg leg. I never knew how he lost his leg, but to us he was "Mr. Peglegger." My friends and I loved to throw objects, like rolled up paper bags, etc., from the bus to unsuspecting vehicles passing us from the direction we were going. We hit the jackpot one day. I found a huge orange that had been left on the bus for several days and it was "overripe." Just as a lady came by at a decent speed, I gauged my timing and threw that "ripe" orange out the window. It hit the windshield right in the middle and splattered over the entire windshield. We never heard from the driver, why I will never know, but I am sure they had bad thoughts every time they passed a school bus from then on.

On one occasion the old bus was acting up, and one of the young ladies on the bus started giving the driver a hard time. He jumped up out of the seat and said, "If you think you can drive any better, get up here." Well, she accepted his challenge and jumped in the driver's seat. One or two of the boys on the bus shouted out, "Let me off, I ain't riding on here with a woman driver." She gave them time to get off and then closed the door, put that old stick shift bus in gear and away we went. I remember seeing those boys yelling, "Wait for me!" Too bad, she drove that bus for a ways and then our driver got back in the seat and we continued our journey.

I was in about the 11th grade when I first went to work on a real job. I took a job for $1.00 an hour bagging groceries at Mae's Discount Center in Orange, Texas. For a long time, I rode a "Mo-Ped" to work after school and on Saturdays. A Mo-Ped was a little motorbike that you could ride by either pedaling it or using the little motor. They would run about 40 M.P.H. and I put hundreds and hundreds of miles on it. It was about that time, my junior or senior year, that I bought my first car. A man I remember only as Mr. Wiggley had a car repair shop several miles from us toward town.

Since I was raking in the big bucks now, I figured it was time for me to have my own vehicle. He had a green 1951 Chevrolet Sedan for sale, and he was asking $40.00 for it. He told me that it had Babbitt rods, and the car would run for a long time, as long as I took it easy with it. Babbitt rods in an engine meant that the rods did not have inserts where they attached to the crankshaft. When the rods began to wear down and get slack, you could take the rod cap off and file down the flat surface on both sides of it and take up the slack and stop the knocking. The car lasted one trip to my home on the river, and it was knocking so loud, you could hear it long before you arrived to your destination. You see, speed is something that is in your blood, and it doesn't matter if it is a boat, a motor scooter or a car, you have to get everything out of it that it will give. Mr. Wigley was a good feller and took the car back and gave me my money back.

My next vehicle was a 1954 Chevy Bellaire 2 door. It was a really pretty car, turquoise, and white. It had an inline six-cylinder motor in it and a two-speed power glide transmission. That car was almost unbelievable for top end speed. I was once trying to keep up with one of my brother's 1957 Ford that had a 312 cubic inch Thunderbird Special engine in it and had 130 mph on the speedometer. I have been in that old 57 Ford and saw the needle on the speedometer go past the 130 mark and lay down and not move. I kept close to him in my little 1954 Chevrolet until he reached 115 mph. My speedometer was showing 112 mph when I slowed down and pulled into a gas station. When I got out of the car, I heard a funny noise and looked and saw that the left front tire was about half flat and going flatter in a hurry. It is only by God's grace and hand upon us that we were not killed in a horrible accident because of the way we drove those vehicles.

I graduated from Little Cypress High School in 1965. It was that year that the Owens-Illinois Paper Mill Company bought all the land on the river where we were living, and we had to move. We had our house moved about 8 or 10 miles to some land my oldest brother had bought just outside Orange in a housing addition by the name of Kinard Estates. I was the only one of the boys left at home when I graduated. Mama and daddy lived there as long as they were healthy enough to take care of themselves. My mother was later diagnosed with cancer of the throat and had surgery. Later on, she was diagnosed with lung cancer and died several years after her throat surgery. Daddy lived by himself for quite a number of years until he developed Alzheimer's disease and couldn't properly take care of himself. He was a few days shy of ninety years old when he passed away at the Jones Rest Home in Orange, Texas.

While I was young, I would often think about losing my parents, and I believed that I could not cope with it. There is a beautiful song that Squire Parson sings titled "New Grace." I experienced that new grace when I was able to attend both my parents' funerals and not shed a tear. It was not that I was hard-hearted or didn't love my parents as much as others do theirs. It was God's grace that gave me the assurance that I would spend eternity with them in Heaven someday. The great Apostle Paul made reference to "the peace that surpasseth all understanding." Grace not only saves us, but it also keeps and comforts us, when no human words or deeds can.

Another person had a great impact on my life that would allow God to use our family in a special way. I have a cousin, John Robert Sims, who was raised just south of Jasper, Texas. Jasper is 20 miles north of Kirbyville, where I reside now. We were very close as kids, and it continued into our adult lives. John was the one God used to get me involved in playing music. Mama bought me a little flat top guitar after I graduated from high school. Both her and Daddy could play a few chords on it. None of my other brothers could then or now play musical instruments. John's daddy, my Uncle Brady Sims, was an old-time fiddle player. I got interested in playing the guitar with John, and we would play rhythm guitar for Uncle Brady. A little later, a few of us kinfolks would get together and try to get a band together, but never really got it off the ground. It was not until I met my wife and her family that I really got involved in music. Since then I have learned to play four different instruments. I can play the guitar, banjo, mandolin and the bass guitar. I am by no means a professional, but my family had some great times singing for the Lord as "The Woodard Family."

CHAPTER III
A Wife and Family

After graduating from high school in 1965, I continued to work in grocery stores. Two of the funniest things I can remember about working in those stores were a couple of incidents involving the superintendent of the Mae's Discount Center grocery stores. There was a store in Orange, Texas and also one in Beaumont, Texas, about 25 miles west of Orange. Our superintendent would make his rounds between the stores. He loved to catch shoplifters. You would be amazed at who would steal, what they would steal and the ways they would carry out their crimes. On one occasion a little boy about 9 or 10 years old was caught red-handed by our superintendent eating a Banana Flip or some type of small pastry. Back then they cost a dime. The little boy was walking around the store eating that pie and our superintendent had him in his sights. As soon as that young man ate that pie and tried to hide the evidence, the wrapper, our superintendent moved in for the kill. He got me, the store manager, and the criminal and we went in the back of the store and into the milk cooler. It was not freezing in there, but it was cold. Our superintendent questioned the young man about "how many of them pies" he had ate in his store. The young man replied, "One or two." Our superintendent threatened to slap him for lying. The criminal's story immediately changed to "maybe 9 or 8." The poor little criminal was told he was going to be left locked up in that cooler all night and the next morning the police were coming to haul him to jail IF HE WAS STILL ALIVE! In all my years, to this day, that is the only time I ever witnessed a human being falling on his knees, clasping his hands and looking into someone's face and saying, "Please don't call the police, I won't ever eat another pie!

The next incident, I found out by noticing our Superintendent showing up at our store with two black eyes and was moving very slow. I asked our store manager what happened. He told me that our superintendent was watching a potential shoplifter while in the loft at the front of the store. He climbed out over the section over where they kept the buggies and fell through the ceiling, hit the buggies and bounced off on the floor. In the process, he broke a few ribs and had two black eyes. Our store manager told it to me this way. "I was looking for our superintendent, thinking he had gone home. The next thing I knew, he came crashing down through the ceiling a few feet from me."

I was working at a Weingartens grocery store when I met my future wife's brother-in-law. He set up a date with my wife's younger sister, who I never dated. When I drove from Orange to Kirbyville to meet my date, I met the "Jewel" of my life. My wife's full name at that time was Jewel Dean Busby, and what a Jewel she was and has been the many years we have been together. We dated for about a year and were married on May 27, 1967. She was eighteen years old, and I was twenty. We were married in a home wedding at one of my brother's homes. At the time we were married, I had quit working in grocery stores and was working as a carpenter apprentice out of the Beaumont, Texas local union. We had two daughters, Rebecca Jane, and Connie Euleen in the early stages of our marriage.

My wife came from a large family also. She had five sisters and one brother. Her father was a self-employed auto mechanic and had his own business. It is almost an hour's drive from Orange, Texas to Kirbyville, Texas, and I spent many hours on the road back and forth seeing her. Kirbyville is a very small town of about 2,000 people, and there was virtually nothing there for young people to do, as far as entertainment goes. Most of our dates involved going to a movie in Orange. At that time, they had a Drive-In movie and we went there often. They always showed a double feature, but we seldom ever got to watch the second feature, as Jewel had to be home in Kirbyville by 10:00 o'clock p.m.

Not long after we were married, I got a job at the American Oil Company in Texas City, Texas as an operator trainee. If a person liked that kind of work, it was the job of a lifetime. The pay was good; it had great benefits and no hard physical labor. One thing I didn't like was the work schedule. We had to work shift work, which consisted of three shifts. We also worked a rotating schedule. That meant that you would work 1 set of each shift with two days off between shifts. What was so bad about that was the fact that the days off were not on the weekends, but were staggered throughout the year. Basically, once about every six months, you would be off on a Saturday or Sunday.

Jewel and I lived in a tiny apartment. We had only one vehicle, and she was expecting our first child. To say things were tough financially then is an understatement. I had to wait two weeks for a payday, and we were out of food, except for dry beans, which we ate every day. I went to work several days without a lunch. We didn't know any friends at that time and didn't have any family there to help us. I was having to catch a ride with a fellow employee, who was Spanish. He was a likable man and never mentioned any kind of problems in his life. He had just bought a new red Volkswagen bug. What came as a shock to me is that he didn't come by to pick me up one morning, and I later found out that he had shot himself and committed suicide. One never knows what is going through someone else's mind.

I continued working at the refinery, and we made friends with a couple that lived near us. The man loved to fish as much as I did. We lived near Galveston Bay, and there was some great fishing. On one occasion we rented an aluminum boat with a small motor and went out into the bay and got out on a platform and fished. I had a big 4.0 Penn reel with about 400 yards of 50 lb. test line on it. I caught a small pan fish and put him on for bait. I hooked what must have been a huge stingray at 9:00 a.m. one morning. When the big stingray made his first run, the line was so far out you could barely see where it went into the water. In fact, when the big ray stopped, the core of the reel was showing. I fought that stingray until 10:55 a.m., one hour and fifty-five minutes and never got him to the surface. I had caught stingrays before and knew their tactics of lying on the bottom and creating a vacuum, making it impossible to raise them up off the bottom. That big stingray would suck into the sand and rest up, and I would fight him again and again. When I finally got him close to the platform we were fishing on, he ran under it and cut my line on the barnacles on the pilings.

We used to go fishing off piers at different occasions. There was one pier going a long ways out into the Gulf. There was an elderly lady fishing on the very end of the pier on one of our trips. My friend went to the end of the pier and cast his line as far as he could into the water. The older lady came up and began screaming at him for fishing too close to her line. She was so furious that she took her big surf rod and began beating my poor buddy with it across his back, neck, head and anywhere else she could find a spot on him. He grabbed his fishing pole, and we evacuated the premises so fast I left my tackle box.

I continued working at the plant and finished my probation period and had all the benefits the company offered. What led to me quitting the refinery took place when I was working one of my evening shifts. My job was to walk around every two hours and take some readings on some instruments. On that night, I noted some instruments were giving some unusual readings and went back to the control room to report it to the operators. Everyone seemed to be in a panic, and rightfully so. They had what we called, "lost the unit." The unit I was working in was the #3 Cat Cracker Unit, which at that time, was the biggest unit in the world. Basically, it is a unit that uses a catalyst to break down crude oil. The oil would be heated, and as it turned into a vapor in a tower, it would go up and start cooling off. The gas off the heavier liquids would cool off first. The tower had collection trays in them where the cooled gas was drawn off and sent to different towers. That night the Debutanizer Tower, the one that collected the butane, had a 5" pressure relief valve blow off of the top of it because of the high pressure. I watched a huge cloud of butane gas go up into the night air. They were dumping all the flammable materials into a flare that had a red flame a couple of hundred feet high shooting out of the top of it. By the grace of God, the wind blew the cloud of butane away from the flare, instead of toward it. Had that cloud of butane ignited, it would have burned that entire unit and everyone in it to the ground. After that experience, I quit, and we moved back to our hometown.

Our first daughter was born not long after we moved back to Kirbyville. There was a little health clinic just a little ways from our in-laws home and our first two children were born there. The entire bill for the doctor and hospital stay was $150.00.

I have tried many different kinds of work in my lifetime. At the time our second daughter was born, I was working for the Engineers for the Texas Highway Department. I worked for the state highway department for a year and finally had to seek work elsewhere. We got paid once a month and made a whopping $300.00 a month. Talk about hard to stretch a check out. It was during that time working for the state that our second daughter, Connie, came down with a bad stomach virus and we almost lost her by the time we got her to the doctor. We had moved to Brookeland, Texas, near Sam Rayburn Reservoir, and had to bring her on a cold and icy night to the health clinic. They admitted her and immediately gave her an IV to put fluids back into her system. She was a very sick little baby, but thank God; she pulled through with no lasting effects of the illness.

I worked for the state one year and left because a family of four could not make it on $300.00 a month. For several years we moved from job to job and home to home, never staying in any place for any length of time. I went to work once for a lumber mill in Pineland, Texas. A supervisor took me back into a building filled with so much sawdust that you could barely see more than a few feet. They had a turntable across from me where two employees would take boards off a conveyor. They sorted them and threw them on the table. My job was to take the boards off the turntable that resembled a small merry go round and stack them on a buggy. When the boards were stacked as high as I could stack them, I was to move the buggy and get another one and start the same job again. Somehow I couldn't see myself making a career out of stacking boards in a building that had so much sawdust in the air you could scarcely see, let alone breathe. The next morning of my new job, when everyone punched out for their morning break, I punched out also. The difference to my punching out and the others is that I punched out for good. I went and loaded up my wife and two kids and headed to Orange, Texas, where I went to work as a ship fitter's helper for Levingston Shipbuilding Company.

I mailed the Temple plant people a letter with mailing directions on where to send my 10 hours pay. That ended my career stacking boards on a buggy. It was at the Levingston Shipbuilding Company that I became interested in welding and went through their welder's apprenticeship program and became a first class welder. The shipyard was located on the Sabine River, and we had to ride a ferry back and forth to get to the workplace that was located on a small island. On one occasion, the barge didn't quite make it all the way to the other side, and an old man jumped off onto the bank. He was trying to beat the rush to the parking lot, in order to not get stuck in the traffic getting out. When he jumped off the barge, he lost his balance and fell backwards into the river. Of course, everyone on that end of the barge almost laughed themselves silly over his stunt.

On another occasion, an older ship fitter stumbled and fell in the crowd of men walking on the barge. He told me that all he saw was boots coming at him. He said they stepped on his chest, head and everywhere else, trying to be first to get on that barge and beat the crowd to the parking lot. He told me that if he had had a heart attack the quarter mile or so up the road where the crowd started, he knew his body would never hit the ground until his corpse arrived with the others to the barge.

On one occasion I watched them launch a big drilling barge. It was huge and people from the media had lined the shoreline across the waterway from the barge. There were all kinds of fancy looking men in suits and ladies all decked out in fancy shoes and dresses watching the launch from their side of the waterway. The barge was launched by cutting flat bar that was keeping it from sliding down greased ramps that angled into the water. They had huge nylon ropes about 2" in diameter, tied to the barge and the shoreline anchors.

When that huge barge slid off into the water, those huge nylon ropes snapped like sewing thread, but finally stopped it. What the ropes didn't do was prevent the barge from sending a miniature tidal wave toward the shoreline across the waterway. I will never forget those classy folks turning and making a run for the safety of the big shop behind them. Guess what, they couldn't outrun that big wave, and it caught up with them and drenched them from head to toe. Of course, we all laughed ourselves silly overseeing such a spectacular sight. I worked at Levingston Shipbuilding Company on several different occasions and could tell many experiences I had while working there.

I later went to work for a company planting trees. We went out in the company truck to a location and were given a little spade type shovel and a bag of little pine seedlings. We would stick the spade in the ground, drop a seedling in the hole, and take our feet and stomp the dirt around it. I found out that they planted trees in the wintertime when it was freezing cold and burned brush in the middle of summer when it was so hot you could hardly breathe. A lot of the little trees were planted while the "planter" sat in a metal cage that was pulled behind a bulldozer. It was only a few inches above the ground. The planter cage would dig a little trench, and you would drop a seeding in the furrow. The dirt would be pushed back around the little tree behind you by a couple of little blades. As we were talking that afternoon after hand planting trees all morning, a couple of the older employees started telling of some of their experiences in the cage. On one occasion the dozer driver had driven over a stump and almost ruined the poor guy in the cage for life. He had just recently gotten out of the hospital from his injuries. Another one told us about all the times they were pulled through bumblebee or yellow jacket nests in the ground and were helpless to defend themselves inside the cage. Everyone took their turn that afternoon except me. I was able to convince them that I would take my turn the first thing the next morning. What they didn't know was that I had already made my mind up that my tree-planning career was going to last one day. I never showed up for another day's work planting trees.

My wife's grandmother lived in a little town called Brookeland, Texas. It was about 45 miles north of Kirbyville. We spent many days and nights there, as one of the hottest bass fishing lakes in Texas, Sam Rayburn Reservoir, is located there. The lake was in its early stages, and you could stop your boat about anywhere in the lake and catch small largemouth bass as fast as you could reel them in. I spent many days fishing on that lake and caught bass by the hundreds.

What we call Bass Boats now were pretty scarce back then. I had a 10-foot Ryan Craft aluminum boat with a 6 HP

Mercury outboard on it. I had no trolling motor at that time. I would sit on the front seat and paddle that little boat from daylight to dark many times fishing. The little Mercury motor would get the boat up on top of the water and scat across the lake good. I can remember going across the lake at times when no one was willing to try because of the big waves and high winds. I went across on one occasion and on either side of me was a wall of water over my head. I would get between the waves and stay as long as I could until I reached the other side and was able to get out of the rough water. On other occasions, I would ride the waves like one on a surfboard would do. I would keep the boat going fast enough to stay on top of the wave and ride it until I was able to get out of it and then catch another wave.

I cannot remember where I found my next boat, but it was 9' 4" long and 44" wide and was made out of heavy sheet metal. I bought a 1965, 20 HP Mercury for it. I did finally get a little trolling motor for it and caught many a bass out of that little boat, as well as spent many hours running up and down the Sabine River where I was raised. On one occasion, a few of my brothers and myself met early one morning in February at the San Augustine Park on Sam Rayburn Reservoir for a family fishing tournament. I had my wife's little brother with me, Joe, who was around 12 or 13 years old. It was very cold that morning, around 29 or 30 degrees. We fished several different places and hadn't caught the first bass. I had heard that jigging a silver spoon just off the bottom in deep water was catching a lot of bass. There was a tree line quite a ways out in the lake and the water was 25 or 30 feet deep. There was very little wind that morning, and I told Joe, "Let's try jigging some spoons near the tree line." I killed the engine and dropped a silver spoon over the side and let it sink to the bottom. The lake was very calm that morning, and the boat was drifting very slowly. I remember feeling something on my line and thought I was hung up on a limb in the deep water. When I tried reeling the line in, I felt a heavy tug. For the next 30 minutes or so, we experienced the most unbelievable bass fishing experience of my lifetime. As fast as we could drop a bait to the bottom and bounce it a time or two, a big bass would grab the bait. We were fishing with small Zebco 202 spin casting reels with 12 lb. test line and lost far more fish than we landed. On several occasions we had bass well over 5 lbs. on top of the water, only to have them break our lines or throw the hook. Had we had some real fishing equipment, there is no telling the amount of big bass we would have landed that morning. When it was all over, we had 12 bass that weighed 33 pounds. We lost all the bigger ones we had hooked. We stopped at a local store, and they took our picture and put it in the Jasper Newsboy newspaper.

I have never run across a school of big bass like that concentrated in one spot again. My father-in-law and I used to chase what we called "school bass." I have seen schools of bass come to the surface that contained hundreds of what we called yearling bass in the 1 to 2-pound range. The bass would be chasing a school of shad and would go into a feeding frenzy. The fish would strike most any kind of bait you threw at them. Most of the time we would use a bait called a "Little George" or a "Hot Spot" that resembled a shad. The baits were heavy and could be cast a long ways, which helped because the bass were constantly moving. My father-in-law and I had been chasing school bass one morning and had caught quite a few. The fish had gone down, and we were just sitting and waiting for them to come up, so we could cast into the school. The fish started striking, and my father-in-law drew his rod and reel back to try and cast that heavy bait into the school of fish. The line didn't release, and it looked like he threw that rod and reel half way across the lake.

He lost several nice rod and reels because of them slipping out of his hand when trying to cast them. He and I spent many days fishing together on Sam Rayburn Reservoir and caught fish by the hundreds and hundreds. Sometimes, later in the day, we would go to a tree line in water about 20 feet deep and fish for Bream. The Bream would concentrate around one of the big dead trees in the water and you could catch them as fast as you could drop a bait to them. We would fish straight over the side of the boat and usually use earthworms for bait. We later found out that whole kernel corn in a can was an excellent perch bait, and one can have hundreds and hundreds of little kernels of corn in it. On one occasion we had used all our bait, and the bream were still biting. We cut off a little piece of a red rubber band and put it on the hook. As fast as we dropped the rubber band down about 6 or 7 feet, a big bream would bite the red rubber band, and we could continue catching perch as long as we wanted to fish.

I bought my first "Bass Boat", which was a little Hustler bass boat. It had a 20 HP Johnson outboard on it and had what was called a "Jim Stick" steering in it. It was 13 feet long and had two swivel seats in it and a trolling motor on the front. My brother-in-law liked to fish as much as I did and we spent many hours' bass fishing on the lake. On one occasion, late one evening, we went out in the little bass boat to do some plastic worm fishing at my favorite wormhole, about a mile or so from the Mill Creek boat ramp. That evening I caught the biggest bass I had ever seen in my life. We had no live well or even an ice chest to put our fish in. I had a new nylon fish stringer that I put the huge bass on and threw him over the side. The fish stringer was a nylon string about 1/8" in diameter with a metal ring on one end and a pointed metal end on the other. You could stick the point through a fish's bottom lip and run the point through the loop on the other end, and the fish could swim around and would stay alive as long as he was in the water. I picked the big bass up on two or three occasions, and both of us would try to guess how much he weighed. I had no fish scales with me at that time, and we could hardly wait until we could get him to a store with some good scales to weigh him.

We fished for several minutes more, and I caught another bass about 3 or 4 pounds. When I picked up the fish stringer to put the freshly caught bass on it, the stringer was empty. The huge bass was gone. Upon examining the stringer, I noticed that the ring on the stringer was not closed up all the way and had a small gap in it, just big enough for the line to slip through. Amazingly, the line pulled through that little gap, and the big bass pulled the ring through the bottom of his mouth, which was tender. I was literally sick! The biggest bass I had seen up to that time was an eight-pounder caught by an old man that ran a boat rental place at Mill Creek Park. I later caught a 7½ pounder and the big bass that I lost off the new fish stringer was much bigger than it. My brother-in-law said, no doubt the bass weighed at least 10 pounds. It was a monster back in those days.

We continued fishing until after dark. All we had was a little flashlight for light. While we were fishing, we noticed it was lightning across the lake, and a small breeze had started blowing. I told my brother-in-law that we had better head back to the boat ramp. The little 13-foot bass boat was flat bottomed and was not good in rough water. We headed back toward the boat ramp and the wind really picked up in a hurry. Water began coming over the side of the boat because the waves were coming from the left side. My brother-in-law shined the little flashlight in the back of the boat and saw that we were taking on water fast. The only thing we could do was to pull the drain plug in the back of the boat and let the water run out. In order for the water to run out, I had to keep the boat planed out on top of the water. It was a pretty scary trip coming back to the boat ramp in the dark, with only a little flashlight and water coming over the sides of the boat, but we made it safely back to the ramp. We arrived, having caught and lost the biggest bass I had ever laid my eyes on.

I also got involved in another hobby on the lake that took a lot of my time. There were lots of Indian arrowheads found along the shores of the lake. My cousin John Robert and I found 75 one evening while picking up handfuls of rocks in water about waist deep by an island near Mill Creek Park on Sam Rayburn Reservoir. The next morning, I went across the lake to a point that extended out into the lake. There were a couple of little high points that were just above the water. It was fairly cold that morning, and as I eased my boat up to one of the little points, I noticed that the water was about 6 inches deep and crystal clear. As I stood on the front of the boat and looked at the small rocks exposed by the waves just under water, arrowheads were everywhere! I pulled my boots off and started wading through the shallow water picking up arrowheads. In a few minutes, I would fill both pockets full and walk back to the boat and empty them in my boots. In a matter of a few minutes, I had 125 arrowheads. At one time I had about 500 arrowheads. I have given many of them away but still have a few hundred of all sizes and shapes. It is now illegal to hunt them in the state of Texas; I have been told. I also have quite a number of pieces of pottery, as well as a few knives and scrapers.

Our family suffered a real tragedy just before our second daughter was born. One of my brother's wife was diagnosed with a brain tumor. The tumor was inoperable, and she passed away at the age of 25 years. She left two very young boys at the ages of about 2 & 3 years. My mother and father helped take care of them, as my brother had to work to earn a living. Both grew up to be successful young men. The oldest of the children, Robert, enlisted in the army and married a lady he met in New York. Toby, the younger of the two, went to New York for the wedding and met his future wife. Toby moved to New York and has been living there for over 20 years. Robert lives in Orange, Texas and is employed by the company I retired from, Southeast Texas Industries, as a safety supervisor.

CHAPTER IV

Entering The Ministry

During the first several years of our marriage, my wife or I never attended church. It was while I was working as a pipe welder for a contractor at a local paper mill that God sent one of many special people into my life. I had a helper we all called "Bo." I was involved in the music business pretty heavy at that time. My wife's younger sister played the electric organ and sang, my brother-in-law, who introduced me to my wife, played the drums. My wife's only brother, Joe played the bass guitar, and my brother-in-law's brother played the lead guitar. My sister-in-law was our lead singer, and we got pretty good at one time. We played at a lot of dances and called our group "The Country Kings" and we really had a good sound. While playing in Houston one weekend, we were approached by a man who told us if we wanted to quit playing for "peanuts," give him a call. We never took him up on the offer, and we quit playing as a group a little later.

I remember giving "Bo" an old Hank Williams eight-track Gospel tape. The more he listened to the words of the songs on that tape, the more he got convicted of his sinful condition. It wasn't long after giving Bo the tape that he was saved. Bo began to witness to me from the time I got to work until I left for home. All he could talk about was Jesus. In fact, the Superintendent of the company fired Bo for witnessing on the job. At that time, March of 1976, I was 29 years old and couldn't remember the last time I had attended a church service. God began to deal with my heart about church and I insisted that my wife take our two daughters at that time, Becky and Connie, to Church. We lived about a quarter of a mile from a Missionary Baptist Church and an Assembly Of God Church. She attended the Assembly of God church first and then attended the Baptist Church. I remember her coming home from church one Sunday morning and telling me that she had rededicated her life to the Lord and joined the Baptist Church. Naturally, she insisted that I go with her the following weekend.

I was still heavily involved in boat racing at that time. Every year they would have a boat race down the Sabine River for about 50 miles, all the way from Bon Weir, Texas to Orange, Texas. A friend and I had taken his 20 HP Mercury and little 12-foot aluminum boat to the Neches River, about 12 miles from my home, the following Saturday. I remember it was in March, and it was cold that day. We were going down the river, both of us sitting on the back seat, when I hit a submerged log. It knocked the motor up out of the water, and when it dropped back down into the water, it caused the boat to throw both of us out on the right-hand side. While under the water, all I could think about was that propeller hitting me, like my brother experienced. I was really afraid to come to the surface, because by all reasonable thinking, the boat should have circled to our right and came right over where we were in the water. When I came to the surface, I was amazed. The boat was 40 or 50 feet from us and running around in circles. The 6-gallon gas tank had flipped up on its end, with the end that the fuel hose was connected to pointing upward. We swam to the bank, heavy jackets, work boots and all, and watched the boat spinning around in circles. In a minute or so, the motor died. It had burned all the gasoline in the carburetor. I swam out and climbed into the boat, set the gas tank up straight and fired the motor up and we took off, with no damage done to the boat, the motor or us. To this day, I do not understand how the boat wound up nearly 50 feet from us while making such a tight circle.

The next day, being Sunday, my wife went to the little Baptist Church, and I stayed home and worked on my boat. She talked me into going that evening, and I felt like a fish out of water. I went with her the following Wednesday night. The pastor preached a full-blown message. I cannot remember what the message was about, but I do remember the illustration he used at the end of it. He told the story of a young man who grew up and found himself in a life of crime. He ultimately was found guilty of murdering an individual during a robbery. He was arrested, tried and found guilty of first-degree murder by a jury. The old judge told the young man to approach the bench for his sentencing. The old judge said to the young man, "Son, do you have anything to say before I pass judgment on you?' the young man said, "Yes your honor I do. The longer I look in your face, the more it seems that I should know you, but can't place, a time when we have ever met." The old judge answered, "Yes son, you do know me. You see, when you were a little boy, you fell into the river and was drowning, and I dove in and saved your life. But today I am not here to save you, I am here to judge you."

The pastor was looking straight into my eyes as this story was told. On that Wednesday night service, with a handful of people in attendance, I walked down the aisle to the front and recommitted my life to the Lord. I was rebaptized, although I know now that God had saved my soul many years before as a young man at Little Cypress Baptist Church. From that Wednesday night on, God began to call me into the ministry to preach His gospel.

Not long after joining the little Baptist Church, our pastor resigned, and the church called another pastor. He stayed a short while and soon resigned. We had an old deacon in charge of keeping the church going, and he would appoint different young men to bring a devotion on Wednesday nights. I believe with all my heart, had I been given the chance to bring a devotional for one of our Wednesday night services, I would have known for sure that God was calling me to preach His word, but I was never asked to do so. I remember the old deacon saying one Wednesday night, "Alright folks, its preacher calling time." The church called a preacher that never really touched my heart with his messages, and I soon left. My wife and I joined another Missionary Baptist Church near Jasper, Texas, with a pastor being one that had preached at my home church a few times. I tried to talk to my pastor and tell him that I felt like God was calling me to preach. His advice was "God doesn't call a novice to the ministry." Looking back, I can see now that he did not understand the difference between someone being called as a bishop or pastor and someone to simply preach God's word.

I had a friend I worked with at the local paper mill who had gotten involved in a charismatic church in Kountze, Texas, approx. 40 miles from Kirbyville, where we were living. The church was located in an abandoned furniture store building, and an older Assembly Of God Pastor was leading the services. The church was a mission of a Baptist church in Orange, Texas. In my opinion now the pastor was not really a Baptist in his beliefs but held on to the Baptist name. I remember the pastor of the little storefront church in Kountze telling me, "If you ever want to preach, let me know and I will let you bring a message." I thought God was answering my prayer through him, and I preached my first message on how Jesus performs miracles. I even said that He had healed my migraine headaches. My first sermon was 45 minutes long. Sadly to say, my migraine headaches continued for many years, and I still have an occasional one now and then. I spent about a year of my life preaching in those churches. I returned back to Zion Hill Baptist Church and surrendered to the ministry and was licensed to preach there. I believe Jesus still heals at His own time and in His own way.

CHAPTER V
First Baptist Church Of Evadale

At this time, we had moved to Evadale, Texas, near the Paper Mill, where I was working. Because of the long drive to Jasper, we started attending Lakeview Baptist Church near Vidor, Texas. We attended there for a year or so until we felt led to attend First Baptist Church in Evadale. They had a young pastor, whom the congregation believed was leading them in the wrong direction concerning faith in giving and receiving. Not long after we joined that church, our pastor resigned, and I was voted as interim pastor. There were many "firsts" in my ministry that took place in my pastorate there. There were also many negative experiences, like at all the rest of the churches I pastored, but the positives far outweighed the negatives, and I will concentrate mostly on the positives.

It was there that I led my first person to the Lord and will never forget it. I remember a lady, "Dorothy" coming down the aisle during the invitation at one of our Sunday Morning services and telling me that she wanted to be saved. I will never forget the beautiful expression of peace on her face after accepting Jesus as her personal Saviour. She was the first person of many that I was to baptize. I was asked over 20 years later to speak at a homecoming at the church, and Dorothy was still attending faithfully. I had the privilege of leading many people to the Lord in the almost two years that I was there. I was voted as their pastor and praise the Lord for the many people that God sent into my life and the experiences I had.

I remember meeting my first missionary, Bro. Cliff Brown. He was the field director of the Bread Of Life Baptist Missions, and he really touched my heart about the need to reach people in Mexico with God's word. I would later make my first mission trip into Mexico with him. I also met Bro. Billy Bridges, who was the founder of the Bread Of Life Baptist Mission. Bro. Billy was an old-fashioned preacher who was a tremendous preacher of God's Word. He preached the first revival for me, and I remember it well. I had just been ordained as the pastor of the church and Bro. Billy had finished preaching the revival services that Sunday morning. When the church ordained me, they gave me a Thompson Chain Bible, and I preached my first message out of it. My text was *Romans 5:1; "Therefore being justified by faith, we have peace with God through our Lord Jesus Christ:"* The theme for the message was that it is possible for a person to be saved, but be out of fellowship with the Lord. During the invitation, one of the deacon's wives came and shared a burden with me. She said that she had been involved in getting a former pastor voted out, and she had asked the Lord many times to forgive her for it, but she could not get peace in her heart. After we kneeled and prayed at the altar, I looked into her eyes and God laid it on my heart to ask her if she had ever been truly saved. She admitted that she did not have the assurance of salvation in her heart, and I encouraged her to ask Jesus to come into her heart and save her, and she did.

After we prayed, I told her to sit on the front pew. When the invitation was over, I asked her to stand up front and also asked her if she would like to say anything to the church. The first words that came out of her mouth were "I got saved tonight." I wish you could have seen the look that came on the faces of the faithful church members. Most everyone broke out weeping for joy, and God's presence was felt like I had never felt Him before. "Jean" shared her testimony and said that she had been raised in a Baptist church and attended faithfully. She was a faithful teacher in our church; she helped during Vacation Bible School and even led some of her students to the Lord. She had a beautiful voice and sang at Rest Homes that she visited, yet she had never been born again.

She shared with us that when she was about 14 years old, she was attending a youth revival with a friend. During the invitation, a lady came to her and took her by the hand and led her to the front, where she made a profession of faith. She told us that she had been living a faithful Church member's life for years. At the time during her true conversion, she was married and had three children, 2 of them teenagers. She told us that no matter how many times she had asked God to forgive her for being involved in having their former pastor voted out, she could never get peace about it. It was not until Jesus gave her the only real peace there is, the assurance of salvation, which she could put her past experience behind her and experience the joy that being a child of God produces.

Her husband shared with me later that he could not believe the change that took place in her life. She had always been a good wife, a good mother and a good church worker. She demonstrated what the great Apostle Paul spoke about in *2 Corinthians 5:17; "Therefore if any man be in Christ, he is a new creature: old things are passed away; behold, all things are become new."* Sad to say, there are many like "Jean" today that are active church members that have not been truly born again and became a child of God. Through the years, I have had the privilege to lead many active church members to a saving knowledge of Jesus Christ. Billy Graham once said that the biggest mission field in the world is the church membership roll. I truly believe that if all the lost church members would get saved in the churches, true revival would come to our nation.

Another great move of God took place during one of our Vacation Bible School services. I was working full time at the local paper mill and could not be with the morning services. One of our deacon's wives told me that if I would do the teaching, she would prepare some refreshments for the young people's class. We would have them during the late evening hours. I told her that I would be glad to do so. The first evening service saw very few of our people attend. After the refreshments, I taught on one of the parables and asked the students to make a list of people that they would invite to the next service. The next night, several of the ones that were invited came to the services. There was a total of 13 people, including the teacher and myself. The age range of the students was from the early teens to the late teens.

After the refreshments and fellowship, I had everyone go into the auditorium and also asked them to spread out over the church. I spoke on the rich man in hell that night. We had a young lady visiting from a sister church that could play one simple song on the piano. As she began to play that song, one by one, a young person would come to me and tell me that they needed to be saved.

The invitation must have lasted for at least half an hour. When it was over, nine of the thirteen present had come forward and asked Jesus to come into their heart. Four of them were the deacon's sons that had made a list out the night before, and five others were visitors. Two of the visitors were an older teen and his younger brother from the big city of Houston, about an hour and a half away. He and his little brother had been sent to stay with his cousins, the deacon's two boys, because he was constantly getting into trouble. He was dressed in black pants and shirt and resembled someone involved in a satanic cult. I remember being told that he had went back home, and he and his little brother had joined a Baptist church and were working on his parents to get them in church. What a blessing it was to see 9 of 13 people born into God's family. The four that did not come forward were myself, my teacher, the little lady that played the one song she knew on the piano and the son of a very wealthy businessman. He stood gripping the back of the pew in front of him, with tears streaming down his face, for about 30 minutes, but would not turn loose and come forward and be saved. I am reminded of the story of the rich young ruler that walked away lost, after meeting Jesus and leaving because he had great possessions.

While there my wife and I were able to attend my first evangelism conference in Dallas, Texas. What an experience it was. I heard Dr. W.A. Chriswell, who was the longtime pastor of the First Baptist Church in Dallas speak. James Robinson preached, as well as Peter Lord, Freddie Gage, Jerry Vines and many others. An Evangelist, Sam Cathy, from Oklahoma, delivered one of the greatest messages I ever listened to. He spoke about the need for bringing the gospel message to the lost because they will not come to the message. He told of an experience that happened during one of his pastorates in Oklahoma. It was about visiting the husband of a lady that he won to the Lord. Her husband's name was Christ Socrates Zovocas. He was a huge man and was a professional pool player. Bro. Sam said that when he arrived at their home, Christ Socrates was in the bathroom shaving, and ever so often he would stick he head out the door and say, "I'll be there in a minute." After a while, the huge man came into the living room and asked Sam, "What can I do for you?" Sam said, "It's not what you can do for me, it's what I can do for you." Socrates said, "Oh, it's this thing about my wife and church." Sam said, "No, it's this thing about you and Jesus." The big man said that he was interested and Sam led him to the Lord that day and he became a faithful member of the church and would go on visitation with Bro. Sam. He became such a great soul winner that Bro. Sam told him he was on his on and didn't need his help.

This is the event as I remember Bro. Sam telling it. It was on a hot Saturday afternoon that Bro. Sam's phone rang at the parsonage, and a voice of one of Christ Socrate's friends was yelling, "I see it, I see it, come over here, I see it." Bro. Sam immediately went to the friend's house and saw him sitting at the kitchen table, bloodshot eyes, sweating profusely with no shirt on and still saying, "I see it, I see it."

Bro. Sam was very excited by then and asked him "What do you see?" The friend said, "I see right here in the scripture that all I need to do to be saved is to call upon the name of Jesus, and He will come into my heart and forgive my sins and save my soul." Bro. Sam said, "Well, let's do it" and they both kneeled down beside the kitchen table where the friend prayed the sinner's prayer. Jesus heard his prayer and saved his soul. At that instant, Bro. Sam saw a movement out of the corner of his eye and saw all 300 plus pounds of Christ Socrates Zovocas crawling out from under the kitchen table. His eyes were bloodshot; he had on no shirt and was sweating profusely. The story is that Christ Zovocas called his friend and told him, I got saved, and I want you to get saved. I'll make a deal with you. If you will read the Bible until you see and understand what you need to do to be saved, I will crawl under the table and pray for you until you see the light and get saved. Christ Socrates crawled under that table late Friday evening and was still praying till afternoon the next day when his friend read God's word and called upon Jesus to save his soul. He had prayed under that kitchen table all evening, all night and all the next morning of the next day until his friend was saved.

That had to be one of the most soul-stirring events of a love for lost souls and the willingness to devote one's self to winning the lost I ever heard. I have told that story many times during messages I have preached. God's word teaches us to go into all the world and preach the gospel. Sadly, most church members today have the "yall come" philosophy. I have heard it said that the average Baptist church member is "saved, sure, and satisfied." They believe they are saved and are sure of it. They are also satisfied with their religion and make no effort to share their faith or win anyone to the Lord. Jesus told Nicodemus that if he expected to see Heaven, he would have to be born again. One of the evidences of the new birth is a joy over an increase in the family. When it doesn't excite a person that a lost sinner has been saved and added to God's family, there has to be doubt about that person being part of God's family.

It was at First Baptist Church in Evadale, Texas that our third child was born. Ruby Annette Woodard was born in 1979. There were about eight years between her and her older sister, Connie. People are very good at jumping to conclusions. The rumor was later spread about me that I had been married before and could not pastor a church. One of Satan's titles is "The accuser of the brethren" and he earned his title well. In fact, I even heard several years later that I was voted out of a church because the church found out I had been married before, which is not so.

God allowed me to stay at First Baptist for almost two years. When my family joined the church, there was about 20 or 25 members coming faithfully and the church was heavily in debt and in the red. When God moved me to another church, we had seen God add over 60 new members and the church was in very good financial condition.

CHAPTER VI
Deer Creek Baptist Church

Upon leaving First Baptist Church in Evadale, I was invited to preach in view of a call at Deer Creek Missionary Baptist Church in Kirbyville, Texas, our hometown. I accepted the call of the church that was located just outside of town. The church property had hookups for a mobile home, which was convenient, as we had bought a new mobile home and were living in a trailer park in Evadale, Texas at that time. We had the trailer moved behind the church, and I started my pastorate there. There were only six people attending the church when I assumed the pastorate. Shortly after I took the church, the family with the two young people left. That left an old deacon and his wife and my family of 5 people, including a new baby, Annette.

I got the church clerk to give me the church membership book, and I started going down the list calling everyone on the list I could contact. Some of the members hadn't attended church in over 20 years and thought it was very amusing to hear from the pastor of a church they belonged to and had not attended in over 20 years. There were two families that did respond to the invitation to come back to church, and they were a real blessing. We began growing at a steady rate as people were saved or others joined by letter. God's presence in the services was tremendous. The water in the baptistery was regularly stirred, as new converts were baptized. On two occasions during the regular monthly business meeting, families wanting to move their membership interrupted me to join our church.

We witnessed another one of the greatest moves of God I have ever witnessed at Deer Creek also. I had heard of a gospel film entitled "The Burning Hell." It was produced by Estus Pirkle from Mississippi. I showed the film one weekend night and the only movement of God, we had in the service was an older man, who jumped up and screamed something and ran out the door during the film. I felt led of God to show the film again at a later date. What we witnessed that night will forever be etched in our minds. Deer Creek Baptist Church was a small country church and would seat about 50 people if it was packed out. I remember that the church was almost full of people, and most were teenagers.

When it came time for the invitation, I had our piano player come and start playing a hymn of invitation, as I stood at the front of the church. There were two young ladies in their mid to late teens from one of the local United Pentecostal churches standing in the second pew from the front, on the left side of the church. They both were standing there, with tears streaming down their cheeks. After a few minutes, they both stepped out in the aisle and came forward and came to me, making professions of faith. They're coming forward "broke the ice", so to speak, and young people began coming. There were so many coming to me that I had to call on every Spiritual adult present to help me deal with so many coming to the front with tears streaming down their faces.

The invitation went on and on, as the altar was full of weeping young people and men praying with them. After about 30 minutes, the last person had come forward, and everyone had returned to their seats. I had no idea how many people had came forward or why they came, so I asked that everyone that had made a decision for the Lord to come to the front. When they all came forward and faced the congregation, they were from wall to wall across the church. There were 25 young people in that crowd that night, and most all of them belonged to a church in the area. There were Baptists, Pentecostals, Jehovah Witnesses and Mormons that were saved that night. As I stood in front of each individual that night, I asked them what Jesus had done for them that night. There were either 13 salvations and 12 rededications or 12 salvations and 13 rededications. It was a service that everyone in attendance will never forget.

As I look back on my 17 years as a pastor, I can now see why God moved me to different kinds of Baptist Churches. The first church I pastored was a Southern Baptist Church, the second a BMA Missionary Baptist Church, the third was an Independent Baptist Church, the fourth was an Independent Baptist Church, the fifth was another BMA Missionary Baptist Church and the last church I pastored before entering mission work was an Independent Baptist Church that I founded, Solid Rock Baptist Church. The churches were located in Evadale, Texas, Kirbyville, Texas, Evans, Louisiana, and Vidor, Texas. I see now that knowing how each of the different kinds of Baptist Churches operates has been a tremendous help in working with all of them in the worldwide ministry I am involved in now.

One of the most precious memories I have to this day took place during my pastorate at Deer Creek. My older brother, who had lost his wife, was living in a small mobile home in Orange, Texas. I remember going down to visit them one Saturday morning. I had planned just a simple family visit, but it turned out far different. We were sitting in the living room talking, and something came on TV that had something to do with end time Bible prophecy. God opened the door for me to witness to all three of them and we all got on our knees around a little coffee table and they all three asked Jesus to come into their heart that morning. They all three came to the Sunday morning service the next morning and made the commitment public, and I had the privilege of baptizing all three of them in the same service.

As most everyone knows, it is very hard to reach lost family members, because they know all about you and have a hard time accepting the fact that you have truly changed. Over the years, I have had the honor of leading several family members to the Lord and praise God for it. I cannot express enough the joy that comes from leading a family member, or anyone for that matter, to the Lord. God's word makes it very plain that nothing touches Heaven like a lost sinner being born into God's family. My favorite verse of scripture has always been *Luke 19:10. "For the Son of man is come to seek and to save that which was lost."* I thank God for Miss Aileen Trussell, who took the time to go out of her way and bring me to Sunday School and church. She has a great reward in store for her because of the many thousands of souls that have been saved because of the worldwide radio and Bible School ministry I am in.

I cannot stress enough the importance of bringing the Gospel message to those outside the confines of the church building. Many people have the idea that a building is the church. The building is where the church can assemble. The word "church" literally means a called out assembly. I remember preaching a revival in a town a few hours north of Kirbyville. We had morning and evening services. The electricity went off before one of the morning services, and it was too dark in the sanctuary to conduct the service. We all went outside under a big Oak tree and had the morning service there. Everyone who belonged to Joy Bright Baptist Church that morning, that met under the big tree, were no less part of the church because they met outside the building. The early New Testament Church did not have the luxury of meeting in a designated building for many years; they met in homes mostly. Even today, Christians in many persecuted countries have to meet secretly to worship God. I wonder how our churches' attendance would hold up today, if we had to meet secretly, because of the fear of persecution, including death?

In the worldwide ministry, I am involved in today, I have received many, many letters from persecuted believers who continue to be faithful to God at whatever the cost. It was not until I founded and pastored Solid Rock Baptist Church in Kirbyville that I made my first mission trip to

Mexico. It was a real wakeup call on how good we have it here in America. Let us never forget the great commission our Lord gave us.

Matthew 28:19-20

(Vs. 19) "Go ye therefore, and teach all nations, baptizing them in the name of the Father, and of the Son, and of the Holy Ghost:"

(Vs. 20) "Teaching them to observe all things whatsoever I have commanded you: and, lo, I am with you alway, even unto the end of the world. Amen."

We had a total of 50 new members added to the church roll, many by baptism while I was at Deer Creek Baptist. We had a great visitation program. Usually, 3 or 4 of the men would meet at the church about 6:30 p.m. and we would gather around the altar and pray for the Lord to guide us in our visitation. We were able to lead quite a number of people to the Lord. Many of those we led to the Lord did not attend our church because of the distance they lived from our church. One thing I learned early about personal soul winning is the object of your going out should be to win people to Jesus, not build up your own church roll. There were times when we would travel as much as 40 or 50 miles to make a visit. I also learned early that unless the object of your witnessing is Jesus, you are not really witnessing for Jesus. As a young preacher, I had visited with older church members at another church I attended in the past and was very discouraged about the way the visits went. On many occasions, Jesus or the church we were from was never mentioned until just as we left. The entire visit would revolve around the weather, politics or maybe the Dallas Cowboys. As we left out the door, the old deacon would hand them last week's church bulletin and say, "Yall come and visit us if you can."

I am convinced that today, as I stated before, by far; most church members have the "yall come" philosophy. God's word makes it very plain in the Gospel of John that the lost won't come to the light, lest their deeds be reproved. God's word also tells us to go out and compel them to come. It has been said that over 95% of the church members in America have never led one person to Jesus Christ. As for me, I believe the number is probably much higher. One of the greatest soul winners in the Bible was the woman at the well mentioned in the 4th chapter of John. In all probability, she was a prostitute because she came to the well in the middle of the day and was alone. I believe this was because the "nice women" of the town would verbally abuse her. God's word says that she went back and told the "men" in town that she had met the Christ. It goes on to say that she brought many people in the city out to meet Jesus.

John 4:29,30,39

(Vs. 29) "Come, see a man, which told me all things that ever I did: is not this the Christ?"

(Vs. 30) "Then they went out of the city, and came unto him."

(Vs. 39) "And many of the Samaritans of that city believed on him for the saying of the woman, which testified, He told me all that ever I did."

I believe unless the main focus of the church is to win souls to Jesus, whether at home or on foreign mission fields through missionaries sent out, that church is missing it's most important function. We know that the Gospel message was first preached in Jerusalem and then spread to other countries. Someone brought the Gospel message to America, and that person was a missionary with a burden to win people to Jesus, not build up their church roll.

I remember during my pastorate at Deer Creek that there was a pastor who came to town that was known for visiting other church's members and talking them into joining his church. He was able to fill churches up everywhere he went, but every church would eventually "blow up" and some would be left with a big fancy building and a huge debt, with a handful of people to try to keep the church going. I have had many people move their membership to churches that I have pastored, but it was because they came and visited my church first and showed an interest in becoming a part of it. There is nothing wrong with having members join from another church, as long as a church keeps its priorities in the right place, winning the lost.

CHAPTER VII

Bible Baptist Church

After leaving Deer Creek Missionary Baptist Church, I immediately became the pastor of Bible Baptist Church. It was the only Independent Baptist Church in Kirbyville. It was founded several years earlier and met in an old store on the outskirts of town. The church had purchased some property a short distance south of town and purchased a double-wide trailer they used for their services. They had built a new building, and it was almost complete when I became their pastor. When I first came there, the church had sold the double wide trailer, and several people were working on it, getting it ready to move or were tearing it down.

I will never forget my first baptism experience there. A middle-aged man had been saved at home and had come to the church requesting membership and baptism. His wife was a faithful member there. I remember starting the water running after the morning service, and one of our men said that he would come back up to the church a little later and check on the baptistery. The baptistery didn't have an overflow and the approximately 6" piece of glass on the front of the baptistery had not been sealed off watertight. Well, as you can probably imagine, my helper forgot about the baptistery filling up. When he came up to the church about 3 or 4 pm, water was everywhere. The baptistery had filled up to the glass and leaked out and ran out into the sanctuary.

The only way to drain the water level down in the baptistery was to get into it and go underwater to the bottom and pull the plug, as it had no string attached to it. He stripped off all of his clothes and climbed over in the baptistery. He dove down and found the plug and pulled it and came to the surface. Just about the time he did, he heard the front door open and heard a lady's voice say. "Sir, is there anyone here?" Some of the people that had purchased the doublewide trailer had left a tape measure in the new building, and the lady had come over to see if it was there. I can only imagine what went through my helper's mind, as he tried to assure her that the tape measure was not there and to get her back out that front door as soon as possible.

It was while I was pastor at Bible Baptist that we had our fourth and last child. Joshua Ray Woodard was born at the local doctor's office before they could get my wife to the hospital. On every construction job I worked, people always called me Woody, as all my other brothers were called. I was working for a contractor at the local paper mill when Josh was born. I remember one of my best friends, who I worked together with for several years, gave Josh the nickname "Splinter." That nickname stuck for several years. My nephew that I led to the Lord, along with his dad and his younger brother, has now inherited that nickname. My dad seldom called anyone by their real name and had a nickname for everyone. I guess I inherited that trait from him, as I have a nickname for most all of my family members and friends.

It was at Bible Baptist Church that I made my first mission trip into Mexico. Two of the men from the church and I drove to Combes, Texas and met Bro. Cliff Brown, the field director of the Bread Of Life Baptist Mission. He took us to some of the churches that Bread Of Life had founded in Mexico. It was quite an experience seeing the contrast in the living conditions of the two countries. I remember meeting Bro. Cantu, one of the very first Mexican National pastors. He pastored two different churches a good distance apart. He did not own a vehicle and caught a freight train and rode between the two churches.

I never will forget a couple that came to the first service we were in at San Iscidro. They arrived very early to the evening service. What touched my heart is that the first thing they did was go to the altar with a little boy who was barely walking. As the couple knelt at the altar, they were taking their hands and helping the little boy kneel down beside them and pray. What a contrast to most church people here in America. Many are constantly late for the services and seldom pray for the pastor or the services.

We had some great services while there. I remember the church being full and people looking in the windows because of the big crowd. Many walked for miles to get to the services. The services seldom lasted less than a couple of hours. I never recall a piano being played in any of the services. Guitars were the main musical instrument used. When the people sang, it came from their heart, and you could tell it for sure. You could tell by their expressions that they took their worship to the Lord as a great privilege. I preached my first time through an interpreter.

We traveled to the other church that Bro. Cantu pastored in a village named El Porveneir. That village was smaller than San Iscidro and the church building was quite a bit smaller also. One thing I remember well was where Bro. Cantu slept. There was a building outside made of cinder blocks that contained a shower stall. The water came from a water tower and was ice cold. There was a double bed frame that had a set of box springs, covered with newspapers on it. No mattress, no blankets, no pillow, just a bedspring with some newspaper on it. I realized for the first time how much many pastors and missionaries sacrifice to get God's word to others.

We met an elderly man that had two oxen that pulled the cart he was sitting in. It was fascinating to watch those oxen pull the cart. The oxen did not have reins to give them directions with. They obeyed their owner's voice commands, like sheep do in Bible lands, even today. Jesus said that His sheep knew His voice and would not follow the voice of a stranger. That same principle should be evident in the life of a believer. Sadly, today there are many "wolves in sheep's clothing" that are leading people astray by the multitudes. God's word instructs us to "study to shew thyself approved unto God." If more people would study His word under the leadership of the Holy Spirit, religious phonies that are fleecing the flock and leading many lost souls to an endless eternity in a devil's hell would not lead them astray.

I had the privilege of leading many people to the Lord while at Bible Baptist. It was during a singing that we had at our church that two men from Grace Baptist Church in Evans, La. attended that would be a special part of my life at a later date. It was while I was pastor at Bible Baptist Church in Kirbyville that I really began to hear God speaking to my heart about going into evangelism. I spoke with Bro. Billy Bridges who said he would pray with me about it, but only God could open the doors for it to be successful. During that time construction work was scarce, and a job was hard to find. After I had left Bible Baptist, I made a sincere effort to get established as an Evangelist, but God's timetable was different than mine. The calling was there, but the time wasn't right.

CHAPTER VIII
Evangelism

After leaving Bible Baptist Church, we went through some really hard times because of the economy. I had four children then, and had bought a 4-bedroom house a few miles out of Kirbyville, Texas. I eventually let the house go back to the seller because of our finances. While there, we experienced some hard times, as well as seeing God do some wonderful things to show us that He was still in complete control. One morning we sent the oldest of our children to school and gave each one of them our last $1.00 bills. I did not have any prospect of a job or any income from anyone at that time. That day when the mail came, our bank statement showed a several-hundred-dollar balance to the good in our bank account. They assured us that their figures were correct, and we thanked God for the unexpected income.

We had a big pine tree just outside the largest bedroom in the house. One day during a thunderstorm, lightning struck that big pine tree and jumped over to the house into the wiring. The lightning burned up the air conditioner, the refrigerator and our compressor and water well pump. I am not sure where we came up with the finances to replace the items destroyed, but I do know that about two weeks after getting everything replaced and working again, lightning struck the same tree in the same place and burned up many of the appliances again. At that time, I almost felt like Job in the Bible.

I had heard of an Independent Baptist Church about 25 miles from home that had Bible conferences, and a preacher friend asked me to go with him to one of the services on a Saturday morning. After I sat down, the pastor, Bro. Jack Walton came and introduced himself and asked me to preach immediately. I have since learned to be "instant in season and out of season" when attending conferences or visiting other churches. My family eventually moved our membership there and stayed there until God led me to another pastorate.

It was while at Anchor Baptist Church in Jasper, Texas that Bro. Jack Walton invited me to go with him and three preachers from his church to California to start an Independent Baptist Church there. They came by my house at around 7 a.m. one Monday morning, and we headed to California in a small motor home. We were going to a town called Buelleton, California, located north of Los Angeles. We drove straight through until we arrived in the town we were to start the church in. Bro. Jack had a brother-in-law in that town who had encouraged him to come and start an Independent Church there.

The trip was a nightmare for me, as I came down with a severe toothache about the second day after we left. I suffered with that horrible toothache for over two weeks. It was not until the third week of the trip that I was able to see a dentist in Colorado to get the tooth checked out. I had intended to have the tooth pulled, but after X-raying the tooth, the dentist said that the tooth was dying. I had the bad tooth filled on the Friday before we left home. The dentist in

Colorado said that the nerve in the tooth was dying and that was causing the pain. He prescribed me some Tylenol with codeine for the pain. What a relief it was for that horrible pain to go away after hurting for over two weeks. I remember that the tooth gave me no more trouble on that trip after taking a few of the Tylenols.

We had planned on having a weeklong revival service in the town, hoping to get some people interested in starting a church. We visited one of the big Baptist Churches the first Sunday we were in California and met with the pastor and told him what we felt led to do. Bro. Jack had rented an old tin paint and body shop to conduct the services in. Before we could have our first service, the Fire Marshall from that city came out and condemned the building for having a public meeting.

What had happened is the pastor of the big Baptist church we visited was a friend with the Fire Marshall, and he talked him into condemning the building as unsafe for a public assembly. The pastor's reason was that he felt like we were a threat to his congregation, although he didn't have enough backbone to tell us he was against what we were doing. He even introduced us to his church family during a morning service. The owner of the building refunded our money. We had already announced on the radio and made posters announcing the services, so Bro. Jack Walton was determined to have the meeting. We set up on the sidewalk in front of the building. I played my guitar, and our Music Evangelist led the singing. Some of the passersby thought it was amusing to see a bunch of preachers from Texas conducting a service on the sidewalk.

We were able to meet a lady that was very interested in helping us start an Independent Baptist Church there. After the trip was over, one of the preachers, who went with us, loaded up his family and moved to that town in California to continue the work started. I am not sure about what all transpired, but I do know that things did not work out, and he returned home not long after driving out there.

The third week we were on the road, we were to preach a revival meeting in an Independent Baptist Church in a small town in Colorado. We drove from California to Colorado, where the pastor had thousands of posters made up that he wanted us to deliver door to door in the town. We walked for miles and miles and delivered those posters advertising the revival services. The best I can remember is that 2 of his members showed up, and we took turns preaching to each other until the last service was over. I found out that Colorado, in all its natural beauty was not very Spiritual, at least in the town we were in. It was evidenced in the lives of the hundreds of people we talked to.

It was not long afterward that the Lord moved us from Anchor Baptist to the next church I would be the pastor of. As I mentioned earlier, two men attended one of our singings where I had invited a Southern Gospel Quartet, The Southern Plainsman to sing. Mackey Willis was originally from near Evans, La. and had many friends that attended

Grace Baptist Church. His friend that was with him that night was Bro. Gary Burton. Bro. Gary has been a faithful member of Grace Baptist Church to this day, and I was his pastor for almost two years. He is still a dear friend.

CHAPTER IX
Grace Baptist Church

As I mentioned in the previous chapter, I preached at Grace Baptist Church on a recommendation by Bro. Mackey Willis, who knew all the church members there. I again saw God do many wonderful things in that little country church. After they had called me as their pastor, we moved into a mobile home that they had used as a meeting place for the church, until they completed a building for a sanctuary.

The first Sunday as their pastor, we went to the Vernon Parish Jail and talked to the prisoners incarcerated there. That was the first time I had ever been inside a Jailhouse, let alone back where the prisoners were locked up. The first inmate I talked to was a young man in his early 20's. He was wearing green army fatigues and had on a white T-shirt. He casually told me that he was facing the death penalty for killing his girlfriend's father. He said him and his girlfriend's father were squirrel hunting one day. I cannot remember the problems between the two, but I remember well the young man telling me that he shot the older man between the shoulder blades with a 20-gauge shotgun.

I recall another young man who asked me on one of our visits, "Bro. Johnny, you people from Grace Baptist, come in here and tell us one thing about salvation. At different times, other religions come in here and tell us something else, who are we to believe?" I asked him if he had his Bible and he promptly got it. I asked him to turn to the following verses.

John 16:13 & 14

(Vs. 13) "Howbeit when he, the Spirit of truth, is come, he will guide you into all truth: for he shall not speak of himself; but whatsoever he shall hear, that shall he speak: and he will shew you things to come."

(Vs. 14) "He shall glorify me: for he shall receive of mine, and shall shew it unto you."

I told him that he could use these scriptures as a guide to know if what he is being told is the truth of God's word. Jesus made it very plain that the Holy Spirit would always glorify Him and not Himself. There are over 300 different religions today in the world. I have heard many people say that it doesn't matter what church you go to because all are trying to get the same place. That is a dangerous way of thinking. Jesus made it very plain that He was the way, the truth, and the life, not one of many ways.

These verses tell us that if anyone teaches of any other way to be saved but through Jesus Christ, it is not of the Holy Spirit. To teach baptismal regeneration, earning salvation by works or any other claim that will get one to Heaven is not taught in God's word.

As I stated before, there are over 300 different kinds of religion in the world today. These 300 religions can be broken down into two simple kinds. There are those who believe they are going to Heaven by what they are doing. Then there are those who believe they are going to Heaven because of what someone else has already done. I told the young man that no matter what religion a person claimed to have, if what they told him did not point them to what Jesus did when He died on the cross, to not believe them. What I told that young man had helped me through the years to know and understand what teaching is of God and what is not. It is very simple; the Holy Spirit does not glorify Himself, anyone or anything over the finished work that Jesus did on the cross of Calvary.

Salvation is not a plan; it is a Man. Jesus Christ can save you to the uttermost. We were able to win many of the inmates to the Lord by one on one witnessing. We did not conduct a service; we talked to them one on one. I was amazed at some in there that were very knowledgeable about the Bible. I was also amazed at the answers we would get from many claiming to be Christians. One man was in there for a third offense DWI (driving while intoxicated.) I asked him if he was going to Heaven and he didn't hesitate to tell me that he was sure of it. I asked him what he was basing his assurance on. He told me that Jesus would welcome him through the pearly gates because he had never done anything all that bad. Another thing about him was the fact that he was a deacon in a Baptist Church.

One of the ladies in the church was faithful to go with us to the jail. Sis. Janis Davis won many inmates to the Lord, both female and male. There was a family living near Evans that was famous for selling drugs and being involved in all kinds of illegal activities. I was told that some of the parent's grown sons had planted marijuana on their parent's land. When the plants were discovered, both of the parents were put in jail in different locations. Sis. Janice Davis led the mother to the Lord while on one of our visits to the jail. She was able to make arrangements to pick "Mary" up and bring her to church services, but she could not go anywhere but to our church. As soon as church was over, they wanted her back to the jail. When her family found out that they could come and visit their mother at church, they all came to church and heard the Word of God preached. I remember leading several of them to the Lord. One of the wildest sons told me after a profession of faith that he felt like he had received a blood transfusion because he felt so clean inside.

There was also a family that lived near the Toledo Bend Reservoir that came and visited our church. There was a young man in his late teens and his mother and stepfather. The young man and his mother both made professions of faith shortly after attending the services, and I baptized both of them. The stepfather did not come to church, even to see their baptism. I remember his wife telling me that she invited him to come to church with her every Sunday. On one particular Sunday morning, she asked him to come, and he said: "If you will trim my hair, I will go with you." All three of them came to Sunday School. While sitting in the

Adult Sunday School class that was held in the auditorium, he suffered a massive heart attack. By God's grace, one of the ladies of our church had some nitroglycerine pills and gave him several of them by the time the ambulance arrived.

Those little pills saved his life. As soon as he was well enough, he came back to church and the instant the invitation was given, he came forward and asked Jesus to come into his heart. I baptized him, and he was faithful until they moved away. He told me that he was planning on going fishing that morning. Had he went out on the lake and suffered the massive heart attack, he would have been found dead in his boat. The stepson I mentioned turned out to be my son-in-law and has been married to my daughter about 30 years, as of this book.

We had many great services there, and I was able to lead many people to the Lord. I made a lot of friends there and probably some enemies. I had Bro. Cliff Brown, the field director for Bread Of Life Baptist Missions, come and speak for us. I also invited another missionary to come and preach who worked with The Bread Of Life Baptist Missions. Dr. Jack Meeks was with us for one Sunday service. Dr. Meeks is the founder of The Bread Of Life Victory Hour radio broadcast that is reaching billions of people with the Gospel. He also started The Bread Of Life International Bible Correspondence Institute as a follow-up to anchor new converts in the word of God. Grace Baptist has always been a very mission minded church. Many souls will be in Heaven because of that little church's support for missions.

Another high point in my ministry was to visit a Bible Conference at Milldale Baptist Church in South Louisiana. The church was huge and was constructed of an airplane hangar. People drove for many miles to attend the services regularly. The Pastor, Bro. Jimmy Robinson, said that on one occasion they were down to 13 members for their Wednesday night services. He told us that they prayed and committed themselves to be faithful to the very end. He also said that if the church went under, it would go under with the people's eyes on Jesus. The church is alive and going strong today. They have some of the greatest Bible conferences anywhere. I remember listening to Bro. Ron Dunn and Bro. Manley Beasley at some of their conferences.

It was during my pastorate at Grace Baptist in Evans, La. that my mother passed away, due to lung cancer. She already had surgery for cancer of the throat and we thought she was going to be OK. The cancer showed up again in her lungs. She took one chemotherapy treatment, and it made her so sick, she said she would not take any more. She passed away after a long battle with cancer. Amazingly, she died of lung cancer and had never smoked a cigarette in her entire life. I was able to attend the funeral and say my goodbye to "Ma" without shedding a tear because of God's grace. I had the assurance that she was a child of the King and that I would see her again in Heaven.

We saw God do some great things while at Grace Baptist Church. I remember putting a little cardboard box on the altar table in front of the pulpit. I told the people that if God really put a burden on their heart for a lost person, they could come during the invitation and write their name on a slip of paper and place it in the little box. We would then constantly pray for those whose names were in the box. My next to the oldest daughter, Connie, had a special friend that she went to school with at Kirbyville. Her father was in the military, and they were constantly moving because of his career. When Connie placed Michelle's name in that little box at the altar, Michelle was in Germany where her father had been sent. Several weeks later, Michelle and her family were back in Kirbyville and Connie was able to have her come to Evans and visit.

God honored the prayers of those who faithfully prayed for the people whose names were in that little box on the altar. God allowed me to lead Michelle and Connie also to the Lord on the front porch of the parsonage we were living in.

Two brothers that were members there while I was pastor have surrendered to the ministry. Bro. Arthur Richmond was pastor of the Sycamore Community Church near Burkville, Texas and his brother, Bro. David Richmond has been pastor of Grace Baptist in Evans, La. for many years. Bro. Arthur also pastored Grace Baptist. As of the writing of this book, Grace Baptist is a tremendous supporter of many missionaries around the world.

CHAPTER X
New Hope Baptist Church

When I left Grace Baptist Church, we moved to Vidor, Texas, where I pastored New Hope Missionary Baptist Church. I believe more effort was put into that church than any before, and we had far less success in reaching souls for the Lord. Both of our oldest daughters were married while I was pastoring there. One of my son-in-laws from Evans and I visited hundreds of homes in that town. We passed out many Bibles and talked to people about Jesus, with very little noticeable results. One of the deacons at the church said that he had a scary experience while on visitation. He had went to a home and told the man living there why he came. The man asked him if he was going to Heaven. My deacon assured him that he was. The man went and got his shotgun and told him that he was going to hurry up his departure there. I had a hard time getting my deacon to visit with me for some reason after that.

I was not aware of it at the time I came to the church, but the church has gone through a lot of problems and had made a bad name. The church voted to change the name of the church from New Hope Baptist Church to Evangeline Drive Baptist Church. I don't think changing the name of the building the church was meeting in helped one bit, as the church grew very little while I was there. I baptized two people in almost two years there. It was not because the gospel was not preached, or people were visited on a regular basis. People seem to forget that the building is where the church meets and it is not the church.

I remember showing the Burning Hell film on a Friday night. We had a fair amount of people that came and watched it. When the invitation was given, not one soul came forward. No one came forward to be saved, none of my members came to the altar and prayed, no tears were shed. What I remember most about that service that night is after we walked out of the church, one of our ladies made a comment about the T.V. program "Dallas." She seemed more concerned about the cast of a soap opera than people going to hell by the multitudes. It is no wonder our churches are not experiencing revival. I have preached many times on the scripture that tells us that he that goeth forth weeping shall doubtless come again rejoicing, bringing his sheaves with him. I heard a saying a long time ago that has really stuck with me. It goes like this. Most Baptists are saved, sure and satisfied. What that says is most Baptist are 100% convinced that they are saved, but they are content with not sharing their salvation experience with anyone else.

I remember an illustration about a young pastor who had taken a little church in the Ozark Mountains of Arkansas. He had gone out and visited all day Saturday trying to get people to come to the services. When he arrived at church the next morning, it was very cold. There was an old deacon there at the church that had come early and built a fire in the potbellied wood heater in the little church. A little while before it came time for church to start, the old deacon went out and rang the church bell. He came back inside and sat by the pastor. Not one person showed up for the services, and the young pastor said to the old deacon. "Nobody has come to church, shouldn't we go and try to find out what is wrong?" The old deacon answered, "Young man, I have already got up early this morning and built a fire in this church. I went out and rang the church bell. Now if they don't want to come, let them go to hell."

I remember preaching in a tiny little church in El Gavilan, Mexico. The church was made of cinder blocks and had a dirt floor and a straw roof. There were 2 – 1" x 12" boards on cinder blocks for pews. A little light bulb hung from the roof for light. It was cold that night. The church was packed with people, and there were a huge number of people outside listening. I preached that night on "Carest thou not that we perish?" The truth in reality is that most professing Christians do not care if people perish in Hell. It is evident in their lives because they make no effort whatsoever to reach anyone or support anyone who does care. God's word says that some sow the seed, some water the seed, but God gives the increase. All believers will be held accountable at the Judgment Seat Of Christ for their efforts to reach the lost. It is our Christian duty to get God's Word to as many people as possible and also do it out of love for what Jesus has already done for us.

CHAPTER XI

Solid Rock Baptist Church

After leaving Evangeline Drive Missionary Baptist Church as being their pastor for about two years, we returned to Kirbyville. It was then that God laid it on my heart to start an Independent Baptist Church in Kirbyville, Texas. Bible Baptist Church had left the teachings of the Baptist Church, and nearly all of the members that were there while I was pastoring had either left or were wanting to leave. There is no doubt God motivated me to establish Solid Rock Independent Baptist Church. How God provided everything needed to establish a successful church is a great testimony of God's ability to meet every need of every church and every person. I pastored Solid Rock Baptist Church two different times for a total of 7 years. I was the pastor there when God opened the door for me to go into world-wide evangelism.

The Solid Rock Baptist Church was started in the living room of our mobile home in Kirbyville. We had a total of 6 people, besides my family, that were considered charter members. We met in my home until we were able to rent an old furniture store building in an alley behind some stores. The old building would seat about 30 or 40 people. We had some good crowds and God really blessed the services. On one Easter Sunday, we had five professions of faith. I baptized all 5 of them in a pond a few miles from Kirbyville. It was soon evident that we needed a bigger building with some rooms for Sunday School classes.

My wife and I were driving around one day and passed the old Call United Pentecostal Church building that was empty. They had built a new building about 3 or 4 miles away on Hwy. 96. There was a sign on the premises from a local real estate agency with a number to call. I called the lady and asked how much they wanted for the building and property. I was told that the property was owned by a local businessman, and he wanted $30,000.00 for the building and 2 ½ acres of land. I told her that I was interested in buying the property. I mentioned it to our church family the following service and they agreed we all should go look at the building. I made an appointment with them for right after church the following Sunday. After the morning service, we drove to the property and found that the building was not locked. When we walked inside, we were amazed how good a condition the building was in. It had new carpet and two new window units. After meeting for months in the small storefront building, the auditorium looked huge to us. The building had four classrooms, a nursery, two bathrooms and an office for the pastor.

As we were looking around, the lady from the realtor walked in, and before we could say a word, she said that the owner would take $20,000.00 for the church and land. He would owner finance it with no down payment at 12% interest. We purchased the church and property and shortly moved into the building. We had four homemade church pews that were made out of 1" x 4"'s and had been used outside at a rodeo arena. Those poor little pews sure looked lonely in that big auditorium. We were able to get enough chairs to seat everyone in them. We desperately needed some church pews.

It was not long until Bro. Mackey Willis, my friend, called and asked me if I knew anyone who needed some church pews. He said the church he was attending at that time had purchased new pews for their church, and the old ones were stored in one of the men's garage, and he needed them moved. One of our member's brother loaned us a truck with a lowboy trailer and filled the truck full of gas. We drove about 50 or 60 miles and loaded the 12 pews on the trailer and brought them and put them in our auditorium. They matched perfectly.

We had an old homemade pulpit that we had brought from the old building, and it looked out of place with that new carpet and fine looking pews. Shortly after getting the pews, a lady that had attended First Baptist Church in Evadale, Texas called me. She was attending another Baptist Church closer to where they were living, Trinity Baptist. The church had bought a new pulpit, and communion table, and she wanted to know if I knew anyone who could use a nice pulpit and communion table. Of course, I knew someone, me!! We went and picked up the pulpit and communion table. It is one of most beautiful pulpits and communion tables I have even seen. The pulpit was made in the shape of a cross and had a matching communion table with it. When we placed it in the church, we saw that it perfectly matched the paneling in the church and also the pews.

We needed a baptistery, as the church people that moved into a new building had taken the old one. The location for a baptistery was there. The company I was working for donated the galvanized material to build a baptistery. I built the baptistery. We had an auditorium that on one occasion had 113 people seated in it. We now had a nice sanctuary, a beautiful pulpit and communion table, new carpet and a big baptistery. We also had four rooms for Sunday School classes. The one thing we really needed was a fellowship hall.

I received a call not long after moving into the building from a brother-in-law of Bro. Mackey Willis. Yes, the same Mackey Willis that attended the singing while I was at Bible Baptist, went with us to Mexico, introduced me to Grace Baptist Church and also called me about the church pews. He was the brother-in-law of the preacher who took his family to California to try and get a church going. He had called and told me that the little church that they were attending had voted to disband. It was a small one-room church building located a few miles north of Kirbyville. He told me that they wanted to donate the building to us. We had the building moved and set up behind our present building. They put the floor levels on the same elevation. We were able to remove a window and make a hallway to tie the two buildings together.

The little church building had two new window units in it, along with new carpet. We built a counter with a top and added a sink, and we had a fellowship hall that was just right for our church. It was not too long that we noticed that the roof on the church needed new shingles. I called a local contractor, and he wanted over $2,900.00 to replace the shingles. As I was working in the shop one day at S. T. I. Inc., one of the owners of the company came out into the shop and asked me if our church needed anything. He said he wanted to give us a love offering, but it was not much. I told him I appreciated it very much. I was handed a check for $3,000.00. Just enough to have all new shingles put on the roof.

One of my daughters, Connie, was a very good piano player at that time. We brought our instruments to church, two guitars, a base guitar to go along with the piano and a tambourine and had some great song services. Our family was playing a lot of southern and bluegrass gospel music at that time. We also had some great singing groups come in from time to time.

It was our family singing group that God used for me to get acquainted with another special person in my life. I had heard about a homeless shelter in Vinton, La., about 50 miles from Kirbyville. I called the founder of the facility, Bro. Burt Stigen, and set up a Saturday night date to come and sing and preach for them. They had a different singing group come each Saturday night and sing. When I learned a little more about the ministry there, I invited him to come and speak at our church. He came on a Sunday morning, and I asked him if he would like to give his testimony during Sunday School and preach the morning service.

While he gave his testimony, there were not many dry eyes in the crowd. Bro. Burt was a combat veteran who had gotten saved while in the military. He later was caught smuggling Bibles into Libya and was put in prison and tortured. He did not go into detail, but we realized we were in the presence of a truly great saint of God, that knew what it meant to suffer for Christ. We have become very good friends through the years. Our church immediately agreed to support his ministry of taking in homeless people and feeding them and helping them get back on their feet. He told me that he didn't broadcast his conversions there, but he said they averaged five conversions a week for three years. If people stayed at the City Of Refuge shelter, they went to church services every time there were services, or they didn't stay.

He turned down a huge grant from the state of Louisiana because they wanted to dictate to him how he could and couldn't run the shelter. They are in the process of building new buildings, replacing the old motel units that were getting very run down. Hurricane Rita hit them very hard, but they are still taking people in and helping them get back on their feet. The most important thing is that many are coming to know Jesus as their Lord and Saviour because of that great ministry. They are using my Bible courses for their studies there.

A few months after going to work for S.T.I. in Buna, Texas I was able to lead Bro. Ronnie Tally and his wife Patti to the Lord at their home one Tuesday evening after work. A little while after Bro. Ronnie got saved; he wanted me to talk to his family. I agreed, and we went and visited them at their home one afternoon. I was able to lead several of his family members to the Lord. They all drove from Mauriceville, Texas to Kirbyville, Texas to attend Solid Rock Baptist Church until the Lord called me into the worldwide ministry. Bro. Ronnie, his wife Patti and their daughter Tosh are presently full-time missionaries in the prison ministry.

I was able to make another mission trip to Mexico with Bro. Cliff Brown and I took Bro. Ronnie, my son-in-law Charlie Goins and my music director, Charlie Ozan with me. God really touched Bro. Ronnie's heart about working with the people in Mexico. God made it possible for him to work with Bro. Rick Shields, a longtime missionary in Mexico.

It was while I was at Solid Rock Baptist Church that I attended my first Mission Conference. Bro. Cliff Brown invited me to the annual Bread Of Life Baptist Mission Conference that was held yearly at Sardis Baptist Church in Winnsboro, La. If you have never attended a mission's conference, you have missed a great experience. It is not only a great time of fellowship with other missionaries; there is great Bible preaching, teaching, singing, fellowship and updates on what is going in the mission field. Sardis Baptist Church has been a faithful supporter of Bread Of Life missionaries for well over 30 years. Only eternity will reveal the many souls that have been saved because of their support of missionaries.

My father passed away also while pastoring Solid Rock. Myself, Bro. Ronnie Tally and my son Josh had taken

2500 lbs. of beans and rice to Bro. Cliff Brown in Combes, Texas. The food was donated by a local church, and we agreed to deliver it to Bro. Cliff. The food would be taken into Mexico and given to the local Mexican pastors to distribute to their people. We made the almost 500 mile trip in the old church van without any problems. Josh had to ride on the bags of rice and beans. When we arrived at Bro. Cliff's in the middle of the afternoon, he informed me that my daddy has passed away around 9 a.m. that morning. We unloaded the food and turned around and drove back home.

I spent a total of about seven years as pastor of Solid Rock Baptist Church. We witnessed God do many great things through His people there. I praise the Lord that the church is still going forward for the Lord. I have many great memories of how God provided time and time again for the needs of the church

CHAPTER XII

Entering Worldwide Evangelism

While attending the Bread Of Life Baptist Missions annual mission conference in the spring of 1995, I was asked by Dr. Jack Meeks to go with him on a mission trip to Israel as a survey trip. He had recently signed on to a new radio station, "The Voice Of Hope Israel." I had never been out of our country except a few trips into Mexico. The thought of walking where Jesus walked and seeing the Bible land with my own eyes was an exciting thought. He and his traveling partner, Bro. Jack Parker, were planning on leaving in August of that year. Both Dr. Jack Meeks and Bro. Jack Parker reside in Huntsville, Alabama, which is about 700 miles from Kirbyville. My biggest concern was raising the funds for the trip.

God graciously provided the funds for the trip through S.T.I. What a blessing it has been working for a Christian owned company. I drove to Bro. Jack's home in Huntsville in an old Dodge van. We flew out of Huntsville to Atlanta, Georgia. We then caught a flight to New York. We flew from New York to Paris, where we spent two days. When we left New York, it was late evening. We flew all night and arrived in Paris just as it was getting daytime. After checking into the hotel, we stayed in, the two Jacks, who had slept most of the flight to Paris, were chomping at the bits to see the sights. I had not slept for about 24 hours and hit the streets with them. They wore me out that day for sure. We saw the Eiffel Tower, the Lourdes where 1,000's of works of art are kept, including the Mona Lisa. We saw a lot of sights in the short time we were in Paris. We only spent one night in the hotel and two days seeing the town.

We caught a subway to the airport to catch our flight to Tel Aviv, Israel. When we arrived in Tel Aviv, we rented a car for about a week and drove to Jerusalem. The hotel we were staying in was located on top of the Mount of Olives. It was named the 7 Arches Hotel. It was dark when we arrived and got checked into our rooms. When you walk out of the hotel, you get a great view of Jerusalem and the Dome Of The Rock. I have many pictures and a great video of our visit there. It was Saturday morning when we walked out of the hotel. The first place we drove to was the Temple Mount. We went first to the Wailing Wall. There were many Jews at the wall that were praying. Dr. Meeks and I wanted to pray also, so went up to the wall and started praying. There was a little wall extending out several yards that divided it from the main wall. While we were praying, we were promptly told to get out of that section of the wall. Women only were allowed to pray there, and neither of us fit the bill.

We spent a lot of time visiting around. There was a Bible museum nearby that had a lot of old books in it. We noticed that tiny pieces of paper were pushed into crevices in the Wailing Wall. People write little prayers on them and put them on the wall, believing that their prayers will get heard and answered sooner. What is so sad about those Jews spending hours and hours praying at the Wailing Wall is that most of their prayers are never heard. Most of the Jews are still praying for their Messiah to come. The Jews rejected their Messiah about 2,000 years ago. How grieved our Lord must be to see the very ones He came to as their Messiah, praying for Him to come.

We visited many touching sights the five days we were there. We drove down to the Dead Sea and swam in it. We went on top of Masada, the site where the Jews held off the Roman army and ultimately committed mass suicide, rather than surrender and be slaves. We drove around the Sea of Galilee, visited Capernaum. We went to the Church of the Holy Sepulcher and Mary and Joseph's tomb. We visited the Garden of Gethsemane. Of course, the highlight of the trip was Golgotha, the place of the skull, where Jesus was crucified. We went inside the empty tomb and saw the spot where Jesus lay. We went inside the Dome Of the Rock. We were not allowed to wear our shoes inside the mosque because it was considered Holy ground. One of us had to stay where we left our shoes, if we didn't, we would find ourselves without any as they would be stolen while we were inside. It was a real eye opener to see the Bible lands and God's Word come to life before our very eyes.

After dark I would like to walk out in front of the hotel and look down on the old city. One night Dr. Meeks walked out with me, and as we were looking down on the old city, from where Jesus had looked down, we had a prayer meeting there. After praying, Dr. Meeks asked me if I would consider working with him on the Radio Broadcast. He wanted me to teach Bible prophecy and also enroll any new students that wrote in requesting enrollment in the Correspondence School. I prayed about it and also shared with my wife what Dr. Meeks had asked of me. I agreed to start working with him in October of 1995, teaching Bible prophecy on a broadcast that potentially reached 3 to 4 million people. Quite a bigger crowd than I was used to preaching to.

I shared the commitment with Solid Rock and told them I would have to start deputation in order to raise funds for the ministry. I resigned the church and started my deputation in the early fall of 1995. I could fill many pages with the things that happened on the road trying to raise support for the ministry, but I will share only a few of the highlights.

First of all, I needed a new home church to work out of. After a few months, God moved us to Trout Creek Missionary Baptist Church in Call, Texas, and a little community a few miles from Kirbyville. God always knows what is best. The Pastor, Bro. Randy Fults, and his commitment to missions and his desire for the church to support our Bible Correspondence School were a tremendous help to us while we were in the early stages of the ministry. The biggest expense has always been postage to mail out the Bible study books. Source Of Light Ministries out of Georgia had been supplying the Bible study courses for several years. The Bible Correspondence School is announced on every radio broadcast, with Dr. Meek's address in Huntsville, Alabama being given for people to write in and request the lessons. The courses were called "The Mailbox Club.

Dr. Meeks would carry the parcels around to churches with him, and the people would mail the parcels for him. He had a lady that helped by grading the tests and assembling the parcels for him. Not long after I began working with Dr. Meeks, the lady that had been taking care of the Bible School resigned. Dr. Meeks brought all the student files to Kirbyville, and we took over the Bible School. There were several thousand students. When we first took over the Bible School, we did not have any support for the ministry. It was after visiting several churches before we knew that God was leading us to Trout Creek Baptist Church.

In the early stages of the ministry, I had a video of our trip to Israel that I would show on a T.V. that I had to carry around with me. We have actually had people make professions of faith during services where I did a presentation with the video. Support was very slow in coming, and we went through some pretty rough times, keeping the mail going before getting the much-needed support from Trout Creek.

Not long after taking over the school, Source Of Light sent a letter stating that they could not keep furnishing the literature free of charge. They said they would have to charge 25 cents for each little booklet. That may not sound like much, but it really hit us hard. While visiting with Dr. Meeks in Huntsville, he asked me to consider designing our own courses. I felt led of the Lord to do so and started designing our Advanced Bible Study Course. It took me two years to put the lessons together. I spent another year designing a Basic Bible Study because I received so many letters from young people requesting studies.

After completing all the study books, I was faced with a new and much bigger challenge. We had to print and assemble our own courses. I had to have a copy machine that was able to print large quantities of lessons. There was also the expense of buying paper and toner for the machine. After buying a used copier from an individual and it not being dependable, I bought a new Konica copy machine from Star Graphics in Beaumont, Texas. The machine was expensive but was a great machine. I used it about ten years and made around a million copies. There was also the task of punching holes in the pages and putting the binding combs in them. I could not afford a good machine. We used a little puncher that would only punch up to five sheets at a time and was hard to use. We then had to put the binding combs in the punched holes. We did that by hand. The combs were inserted in the holes, one hole at a time. I have witnessed some people spend several minutes trying to get one comb in a book and finally give up. Needless to say, it was a very time-consuming ministry, and I was still working full time at STI.

I had some very touching experiences while on deputation. I will share a few of them. I was in a church in Corpus Christi, Texas for a Sunday morning service. I set up a table at the back of the church with some of the ministry items on it. I had a box containing about 30 or 40 packages that needed mailing. I did my presentation during the Sunday School hour and preached the morning service message. After the service, we went into another building for a meal and fellowship. Not one person picked up the first package. Back then a set of lessons could be mailed for about a dollar.

While in the fellowship hall, a Spanish lady in her late 40's or early 50's came up to me and asked me if I would come and talk to her. We went back into the auditorium where the mail was in a big box on the table. She asked me how much it would cost to mail one of the parcels. She got out a pencil and paper and did some figuring. She wanted to mail the entire box of mail. She asked me if I would hold a postdated check for her because she was on a "fixed income." No doubt she was very poor. I held that check for her so she could mail those lessons. I am always reminded of the widow's mite when I remember her; she is special.

At a later date, I was in a Sunday evening service in Lone Star, Texas. After doing the presentation, I could tell that the pastor was not interested in the ministry. He said very matter of factly, "If any of you want to mail one of these parcels, you can pick one up after the service." I remember an elderly lady coming down the aisle using a walker. A young man was with her. I'll never forget her words to the young pastor, "Sonny boy, don't you worry about that mail, I am taking care of it." She had the young man get the entire box, and she took it with her to mail. We need to remember that God does not look at what we give as much as He looks at what is left after we give.

On one deputation trip, I traveled through five states and had to leave my car broke down in Huntsville, Alabama and rode home with Dr. Meeks, who was coming to Texas. I had a box of mail with me and had to bring every one of those parcels back home. But through all the ups and downs, we have never had to turn down a request for study materials because of lack of postage expense.

On one deputation trip, I preached on a Sunday night service in Tennessee. When the pastor gave the invitation, I was surprised to see my youngest son coming to the front. The Lord saved my only son that evening in Tennessee. He was a teenager and had made a profession of faith and been baptized at an earlier age, but discovered he was not truly converted at that time.

Besides designing our own courses, I designed several Gospel tracts, of which thousands and thousands have been mailed overseas, with many returned signed, showing salvation testimonies. I printed these tracts and they were cut and folded by hand by different church members for several years before I got a folding machine. For many Wednesday night services, the people of my churches have cut and folded thousands and thousands of tracts.

Another vital part of this ministry is sending out Bibles to those who cannot afford one. I was shocked to learn that a Bible cost $10.00 in Nigeria, but the average family income is $15.00 a month. How many Bibles would be lying around unopened and unread in homes in America if they cost 2/3 of a month's pay? For many years, I could mail Bibles and other literature in an "M-Bag". They were large canvas or plastic bags that you could put up to 60 pounds of materials in. That ended several years ago when the Postal Service made it mandatory to mail everything overseas by airmail. Postage expense skyrocketed overnight. It basically shut us down sending out large quantities of tracts or Sunday School books, etc. It now costs many times more to mail one Bible, but we continue to send as many as we have the finances to do so.

I was invited to go on a trip with Dr. Meeks to Australia the next year after I began working with him. It was great to see Australia and be in church services there. Sadly, I came down with a severe migraine headache the day we arrived and spent that day and the next bedridden with it while the others saw some of the great sights. The morning before we left Melbourne for Sydney, I woke up with another migraine and kept it for many hours. I went over 40 hours without sleep and was very sick coming back. I do not regret going, as I have some great photos and memories. I was able to learn a lot about the churches there. I have quite a number of students in Australia enrolled in our school at the present.

I used to send out emails to different churches telling about the ministry we were in. I became acquainted with a preacher in Mesquite, Texas that would prove to have a tremendous impact on the Bible School. Dr. Ron Schultz spoke to his pastor of Macedonia Baptist Church and set up a date for me to come and do a presentation of the ministry.

I had a display at the front of the church that I used during my presentation. After the service, quite a number of people came and looked at our materials and asked questions. Dr. Ron picked up one of my Advanced Courses, looked at me and nodded his head. I was not sure what his intentions were, but I found out very soon. He set up a free website for me and emailed the link to me.

The response to the website has been extraordinary. We now have students in over 110 foreign countries and all 50 states here in America. I recently made the lessons available by email and also on a C.D. Dr. Shultz made a tremendous contribution to this ministry by his computer knowledge. Many of our students enroll by the website. We still enroll people that respond to the radio broadcast, some write in and others, even telephone us requesting our lessons. God knows exactly what we need at exactly the right time and is faithful to provide that need at His appointed time.

As our school grew in numbers, printing the courses became more and more of a challenge. I began to have some minor problems with the Konica copy machine. It was a great copier that copied 33 copies per minute. I was able to get an appointment with the owner of Star Graphics concerning an issue with the Konica machine. My wife and I drove to Beaumont, Texas, about 50 miles from Kirbyville, and met with the owner. It did not take me long to find out he was a dedicated man of God who loved the Lord and had a heart for missions. When I showed him the courses we were printing up, he said you need a bigger machine. He took us out on the showroom floor and showed us a Risograph Copier. The machine can print up to 120 copies per minute. He donated a nice machine to the ministry and had it delivered to our home. We had two rooms of our home turned into offices for the ministry.

Not only has he donated the Risograph machine to us, but he has also since donated other machines. Not only has he donated other machines; he furnishes all the paper, toner, ink and maintenance of all the machines. When I became involved in this ministry, I was expecting support to come from those who gave money to the ministry. It never dawned on me that God would provide materials and equipment. It would be hard to put a monetary value on the support from Stargraphics. I praise the Lord for allowing me to meet Bro. Paul Skinner, the owner and become friends with him. Many thousands of Bible Courses and Gospel tracts have been printed on equipment that the Lord provided through Stargraphics and many souls will be added to their account in eternity.

There are many who have helped this ministry reach where it is today. Bro. Cliff Brown once preached at Solid Rock Baptist Church and said: "Little is much if God is in it." No truer words have ever been stated. I have learned that God's provisions for this ministry is like the water in the well that my cousin John Sims got their water from. You could drop a bucket down into that well and pull it up with a rope on a pulley. The water never ran out, and it never flooded the home place. God supplies our need, not needs. We have but one real need that is to be where God wants us, doing what God wants, and doing it out of a heart of love for what He has done for us.

We spent about five years at Trout Creek Baptist Church before the Lord moved us back to Grace Baptist Church in Evans, La. Bro. David Richmond has been pastor for over ten years. He was a faithful member while I was pastoring there. I know of no church that is more mission minded than Grace Baptist. Every year they have a faith promise mission conference. The amount of finances that comes in and goes out to support missionaries is almost unbelievable for a little country church with a few families, all plain country folks.

I have found that I fit in better in Independent Baptist Churches than others, although I have been involved in other Baptist works. I have great friends from every church I pastored and have no regrets about going to or leaving any of them. God has a perfect plan for every child of God. What many believers need to learn is that the same God that called them into His work will lead and guide them in the right direction.

It never entered my mind that someday a poor little kid who was raised on the banks of the Sabine River would preach and teach multitudes. In God's wisdom, he led me to assume the responsibility of the Bible Correspondence School. Dr. Meeks was able to take the resources he was putting into mailing courses and buy more radio airtime. From the time I began working with Dr. Meeks, the potential listening audience has increased from a few million to approx. 3 to 4 billion people! I am a regular speaker on the radio broadcast with Dr. Meeks. God's word teaches us that where there is no vision, the people perish. Our vision is to keep buying more airtime until Dr. Jack Meeks or my voice can be heard anywhere in the world.

A great honor was bestowed on me February 14, 2005, at a mission conference at Bible Baptist Church in Silsbee, Texas. Bible Baptist is the headquarters for The Bread Of Life Baptist Missionary Fellowship. An honorary Doctor of Divinity Degree was bestowed on me by the founder of The Bread Of Life International Bible Correspondence Institute. From March of 1976 when I walked down the aisle of Calvary Missionary Baptist Church to the present, I have been a fervent student of God's word. God's Word teaches that we are to study to show ourselves approved unto God. I consider it an honor to be used of God in the capacity that He chose.

I take pride in how God has blessed me with the knowledge He has bestowed on me. This knowledge does not come by just asking God for it; it comes by being a faithful student of God's word. I have many great testimonies from students around the word as to how God is using our Bible Study courses.

I thank God for all the special people that He put in my life through the years. Each and everyone has a special place in my heart. I have to give credit for the success of this ministry to where it is due. Until December of 2008, I have had to hold down a full-time secular job to provide for my family. Thank God for a faithful wife that has spent hours and hours grading tests, assembling parcels, mailing parcels and every other task that was necessary to make this ministry what it is today.

I also give credit to the faithful prayer partners of this ministry. I know for a fact that we have people from all over the world regularly praying faithfully for this ministry. I realize that when a person prays the way they need to pray, everything else will line up in their life. Those who support this ministry with their finances are making it possible for us to reach multitudes with God's word. Jesus has been with me every step for over 50 years since that little "kid from the river" walked the aisle one Sunday morning in Little Cypress Baptist Church and was saved by God's marvelous grace. The same grace that saved me leads me and keeps me. There are many people that God placed in my life that influenced me. I would like to finish this book with a few scriptures about being used of God.

Philippians 2:13 "For it is God which worketh in you both to will and to do of his good pleasure."

Philippians 2:5 "Let this mind be in you, which was also in Christ Jesus:"

Romans 12:1 "I beseech you therefore, brethren, by the mercies of God, that ye present your bodies a living sacrifice, holy, acceptable unto God, which is your reasonable service."

Romans 12:2 "And be not conformed to this world: but be ye transformed by the renewing of your mind, that ye may prove what is that good, and acceptable, and perfect, will of God."

John 14:23 "Jesus answered and said unto him, If a man love me, he will keep my words: and my Father will love him, and we will come unto him, and make our abode with him."

Ephesians 3:20 "Now unto him that is able to do exceeding abundantly above all that we ask or think, according to the power that worketh in us,"

Chapter XIII
About This Ministry

The ministry we are involved in consists of sending out free Bible Correspondence Courses, Gospel Tracts, Bibles and other Christian materials as the Lord provides us the resources to do so. There are a total of seven sets of lessons that I designed in the course.

The lessons are as follows:

Course 1   Salvation

Course 2   The New Testament Church

Course 3   The Holy Spirit

Course 4   Satan

Course 5   Prayer

Course 6   Death And Judgment

Course 7   Soul winning

We send all our materials out free of charge. The tests are to be taken and returned to us for grading. All of the books are for the student to keep and use as the Lord leads them to do so. A diploma is given upon successfully completing all the lessons.

We have students in over 110 foreign countries and all 50 states in America.

We draw no salary for this ministry; we operate solely by love-offerings from churches, individuals or businesses.

The Bread Of Life Victory Hour

Is Broadcast On The Following Stations

DX Radio Network Stations
Russia - 1 - Serving Eastern Europe & the Russian Federation
Russia - 2 - Serving China, the Russian Federation & Asia
Russia - 3 - Serving the Russian Federation,
Asia and the Middle East
Russia -4 - Serving the Russian Federation, Asia and Africa
Russia - 5 - Serving India, Asia, the Russian Federation and the near East
Russia - 6 - Northern Polar Region, Russia
Russia ï¿½ 7 - Eastern Region, Russia
Russia ï¿½ 8 - Uzbedistan,Kyrgystan
Turkmenistan & the Russian Federation
Republic of GeorgiaGeorgia
Armenia &Azerbaijab
Argentina - Latin America
Boliva - Boliva
Brazil ï¿½ 1 - Latin America
Brazil ï¿½ 2 - Brazil
Brazil ï¿½ 3 - Brazil
Brazil ï¿½ 4 - Manaus

Region of Brazil
Chile - Chile
Columbia ï¿½ 1 - Latin America
Columbia ï¿½ 2 - Latin & Central America
Paraguay - Latin America
Peru - Latin America
Uruguay - Uruguay
Venezuela - Latin & Central America
Leidya Swara - Bandung, Indonesia
Dimensions - Sambuco, Italy
Radio 101 - Rolyatti, Russia
DX Domestic - Brazil
Radio Gaeta - Gaeta, Brazil
Europa Plus - Sochi, Russia
Europa Radio - Various Italy
Voice of Freedom - Bogdanovicha, Russia
Radio Comunitaria - Langus, Argentina
Cultura y Christina - Birigui, Brazil
Voz Sereia - Quixeramobim, Brazil
Viva Jesus - Retalhuleu, Guatemala
DX-1 Relay - Birobidzhan, Russia
DX-2 Relay - Omsk, Russia
Radio DX - Corsera, Boliva
Radio Tiraque - Tiraque, Boliva
Radio Suaracitrah - Purworejo, Indonesia
Bahassa Indonesia - Various, Indonesia
DX Relay - Iriyan Jaya, Indonesia
Network 6 (14 sta.) - North Italy
Radio International - Various Italy

Kazan Solei Radio - Bilyarsk, Tatarstan
Radiostantslya Omsk-2 - Mira Oblast, Russia
Radio Centro (6 sta.) - Various, Urguay
Radio Super Uno - El Alto, Boliva
Sentimental Radio - Nova Xavantina, Brazil
Radio Voz de Verdad - Vila Pocota, Peru
DX-1 Relay - Tura, Russia
DX-3 Relay - Balti, Moldova
DX-1 Relay - Pskov, Russia
Radio Cultural Int. - Acopira, Boliva
Nova Estereo Cable - Pto, Belhas, Brazil
Antares 1 - Sidorjo, Indonesia
DX Relay - Iriyan Jaya, Indonesia
Ray Power - Bauchi, Nigeria
FM 77 - Istriniya Ob., Russia
Santa Clara Radio - El Alto, Boliva
XEMI Festival - Urupan, Mexico
DX-1 Relay - Khanty/Mansiyst, Russia
Local And Cable Affiliates:
Radio Frontera - Yacuiba, Boliva
Cable Radio Uno - Various, Brazil
Lintas Triaga - Bukittinggi, Indonesia
Europa Plus - Sochi, Russia
Avtoradio 2 - Solikamsk, Russia
Radio Severo - 5 - Vladikavichaz, Russia
Radio Noventa - Mamore, Boliva
Suara Stero - Indonesia
Radio Bima S. - Kebumen, Indonesia
Independent Radio Stations:

Philippines Radio - Philippines

Honduras Radio - Honduras & Central America

Radio Anquilla - Anquilla and the Caribbean Islands

Voice Of Hope Israel - Israel, Jordan,
Lebanon and the Middle East

Radio Africa - The African Continent

Voice of Hope Asia - China

The House Of Bread - Bethlehem, Israel

CHAPTER XIV

Student Testimonies

Below are letters from a few of my students. Their names and address have been omitted for their privacy and protection. Many of our brothers and sisters in Christ suffer great persecution for their commitment to Jesus. I have hundreds and hundreds of letters from persecuted believers asking for prayer and help, as they continue spreading the Gospel, even at the risk of their very lives.

~~~~~~

Dear Dr. Woodard D-D

My heart is filled with gratitude; I am truly overwhelmed. I can't believe I actually did a Bible Correspondence Course. I did the best I can. I always wanted to do this, but finances would not allow me. I must say, God's richest continued blessings to you and yours. I must confess also when I realized I had finished, tears came to my eyes, tears of joy and satisfaction. From the depths of my heart, God bless you.

<div style="text-align: right">

Yours in Christ:
Trinidad, West Indies
You have made me a better person.

</div>

Dr. Johnny Woodard
The Bread Of Life Institute
Kirbyville, Texas

Dear brother in the Lord:

Greetings in the love of Jesus Christ, the founder, and maker of love. He first loved us and gave His life for us and make us to copy from Him. Thank God for His love, kindness and compassion toward the world.

Happiness behind sorrow.

Happiness comes when we started your lessons, the way you present your good presentation of the gospel made us move into remote pagan villages, where they believe in their father's idols of wooden gods. We went to idol god worshippers' villages, just to present to them the good news of Jesus Christ and free salvation that He gave to all who believe in Him, who do not need goats and hen's killing anymore. God, in the free pardon of sin, has purchased them by the blood of Jesus Christ. If anyone accepts Christ Jesus as his or her personal Saviour, they are free from sin.

Hearing this, many accepted Jesus Christ by lifting their hands, and we gave them an invitation to come out. We told them that they will not worship idols anymore, and they will not kill any goats and hens anymore for their idol gods. That is when the riots started; some of us were beaten to death because we wanted to destroy their father's false god. Please pray for us, we are ready to go back to the villages when we are well. Please pray for us and the villages, to help us win them for Christ Jesus.

We are using your teaching to prove to the villagers that God is still in action. Please, we like your teaching, is your church teaching the same also? How many students do you have in Nigeria? We want to follow your teaching; it is easy to understand. No church here will accept this pure truth teaching. When hearing from you, we will write more. Thanks for your good teaching. Thanks for love and kindness. Please be with us to spread your teachings.

Yours in Christ

Notice:

We accept to die for Christ sake, for His true teaching, that has not mixed the name of God with idol gods. We are to point out to them the truth about God and the gods of wood. We want them to know that God Almighty is the maker of the earth and all things that are on the earth. We did not have the right teaching to lay our hands on. But now, your teaching shows us the right teaching. Please, please, be with us. Let the light shine in darkness.

Write us soon

Nigeria, West Africa

~~~~~~

Dear Brethren:

I sincerely thank you for the thoughtfulness and diligent kindness in sending me the materials I got from your prestigious Biblical Institute. No words can express my deepest gratitude to you for the assistance you've been giving me by sending the two books of God's word. Whenever I read the books, I feel a fresh fire or zeal and commitment to follow Jesus, to love Him and to love all mankind. Your books, which you sent me, stand for the big part of my Spiritual growth and maturity. It has been a blessing to me, and now I thirst and hunger, yearn for it like physical food because it is infinitely nourishing.

I praise the Lord for your ministry of Jesus Christ. I don't want to be obedient in a religious way as the Pharisees were, but I want to be obedient from my heart with love. Keep pressing in, keep spreading the word, keep walking in love and I will keep you before the throne of grace. I'm thankful to every one of you in nurturing my soul. Christ gives me a continuing life of service and strengthens me to stand firm in bad situations. Please pray for me because I am jobless.

My offering for what you are doing in my sincere prayers is that God will supply your needs. I believe that soon I'll be able to do more than this. May our Heavenly Father, bless you with grace and your worldwide ministry abundantly. In anticipation of an early reply, I'm looking forward to hearing from you soon.

Algeria

Dear Dr. Johnny Woodard:

A warm "hello" to you my brother in Christ.

I am 15 years old. I was born last December 29, 1992. I'm the second oldest child in our family. I'm very thankful to God because I have been given the opportunity to be a student through your correspondence school. If you only knew, the great change that has happened in my life. Bible reading becomes our hobby. I and my younger brothers and sisters became knowledgeable in God's word. Reading the great Bible question and answer book from the Old and New Testaments woke an interest. Praying every day is part of our daily life. I'm sorry if I mail this test back to you delayed. It's just because I don't have enough money to pay for the delivery of my letters to the post office. I need to look for a job here to pay the delivery bill given by the postman. Most of our fellowmen are suffering poverty that even buying our needs, like clothing, slippers, and rice, we can't afford to buy anymore. I hope you understand our situation and will keep us in your prayers, as we press forward for God's work.

I include my picture so that I may have a picture in your photo album. I'm looking forward to the Advanced Course 2 (The New Testament Church) so that I can finish all the course and receive my diploma immediately. I'll close this letter here. Hope to hear from you soon.

Always
Philippines

Dr. Woodard,

Praise GOD!!!

We have received the lessons you sent us and havebeen blessed in our daily devotions and study. As we were reading them, some of our fellow believers have expressed interest in studying as well. Would you allow us to photocopy the material you have sent us?

Your fellow servant,
The Philippines

~~~~~~

Greetings in the Name of our Saviour Jesus Christ!

I am happy to inform you that I already finished the Advance course study you've sent last year. Really, it's a blessing for me to have the opportunity to study and be a part of your Bible Correspondence Course. I already sent my answer sheets last week, and I am sorry for I haven't sent them earlier.

Thank you so much for helping me study the Word of God in a deeper sense. Somehow it answers the many questions I have in life. I would like also to inquire if I can take your Basic Bible Course as well? I am looking forward to hearing from you very soon.

Again, thank you so much and may God continue to bless you and your ministry richly. I will be praying that the Lord will continue to sustain and use your Bible Correspondence Course in helping many Christians to have a better understanding in the Word of God and God Himself and in reaching out many people who still don't know Christ in their lives. Your booklets are great, and I find it very helpful.

Yours in Christ,
The Philippines

~~~~~~

The Lord Bless:

I am so much happy to info you that the diploma you sent is at good hand, may the good Lord meet all your needs. I am so much thankful to the Lord for making it possible for me to go through this course; praise be to His name. Stay blessed in Jesus name,

Love from:
Ghana, West Africa

~~~~~~

Dear Johnny

I wish to thank the Lord for making it possible for us to go through this Bible Correspondence Institute with the help of the good Lord with success. In fact, this lesson has given me a great eye opener into the word of God. Also, I have learned new things in this lesson, which will help me in my mission work and church planting.

In fact, I have just started a new church in one of the new communities in Tema. So far I have (6) six disciples, so I hope to start Sunday services on the first Sunday of February 2008, so keep us in your prayers.

Please, I have given your email address to a pastor friend in Liberia to write to you for the lessons. I hope you like it.

I am so sorry for the delay in sending in the last lesson for I went on a long mission trip and am now back to start a new church.

May the good Lord bless all that you are doing and meet all your needs. The soul-winning lesson was great. It is helping us train people to win souls for the Lord.

Ghana, West Africa

~~~~~~

Dr. Johnny Woodard D.D: President
The Bread of Life International
Bible Correspondence Institute
PO Box 334
Kirbyville, Texas 75956 USA

Dearest in the Lord,

Object: COMPLETION OF THE ADVANCED COURSES AND INFORMATION

I continually praise the Name of the Lord for the tremendous work He has been doing through your Institute to equip the children of God with the Word of God and to spread the Gospel of Salvation throughout the world. May He continue to bless and strengthen you so that the Word can reach the more remote and unreachable places of the earth. Amen!

141

In fact, one month ago, I received some manuals (Advanced Courses 1-7) from your Institute as a student, and I can affirm that these courses have been a blessing for me and the church I have the honor to pastor. This is to inform you that I have now completed all the courses and I will mail them to you tomorrow. And I will be expecting my diploma. Sorry for not having sent you the tests earlier. It was due to the fact that my schedule was very tied...

Furthermore, the main purpose for writing you this note is to inquire about:

The possibility for us here to get a French translation of your manuals because we are in a French speaking country, and our people hardly speak English. In case this option is not possible, can we be granted the opportunity and privilege to get it translated into French for having a wider attendance (people enrolling as students). ·

I would also like to know whether you are not interested in Creating a Regional Branch of The Bread of Life International Bible Correspondence Institute for French speaking people here in Côte D'Ivoire (West Africa) so that as many students as possible can profit from the so precious lessons contained in your various manuals (both Ordinary and Advanced Levels)

I will be looking forward to hearing from you very soon.

Côte D'Ivoire, West Africa.

I wish to thank you for your usual co-operation in the Lord. God bless you and continue to strengthen you for all you do to spread the Gospel everywhere.

~~~~~~

Dear Dr. Woodard,

Heavenly greetings in the name of the Lord. I trust that all is well with you. I received the Course materials on Friday and am writing to say big thank you. I've finished reading thru the WITNESSING, and I even quoted portions in my Sunday sermon at church. What a great support... Today, I started studying and answering the questions on SALVATION. In our part of the world, we don't get such materials easily, and even the cost involved is so much that some of us can't easily buy...This isreally SOLID MEAT. For example, the portion about the Trinity is so simple and that I can now conveniently preach it to the understanding of any person.

Thank you.

I wish to assure you and the brethren who support your ministry that they should continue to do it because only God knows the impact this material has on humanity... including pastors and their congregations. Doc, I have THREE leaders in my church who are true disciples, and I would like to get copies for them, and I will help them to study. Again below are addresses of some of my pastor friends who are also interested:

Nigeria, West Africa

Greetings,

I have just received the diploma you awarded me. I just wanted to say thank you and may God bless you. Maybe you would like to hear a little how I studied and completed your studies, glory to God. Let's see, I studied way way way (not a typo) into the night in some cases. I took them everywhere with me, and whenever I had the time, I would sit down, ask God for guidance and begin. This included times when I would stay overnight at church. I would get up early in the morning, I Even took them to summer church camp with me, hard to see a brother in the woods, studying to the glory of the Lord! I was deeply enriched by the study; I especially loved the study of the New Testament church. I pray God will be merciful enough to use me in anything He sees fit, and I am glad I had the chance to gain valuable tools for His ultimate victory! To Him be the glory and the power forever AMEN!

God Bless your ministries until the rapture!
Hiroshima, Japan
Be bold, trust God.

Appreciation goes to The Bread Of Life International Bible Correspondence Institute for offering me this course, and I pray God bless you abundantly. I will not remain the same in witnessing Christ to the nation and this people around me.

Thanks:
Gulu, Uganda-East Africa

~~~~~~

Greetings in the name of our LORD and Savior JESUS,

I have a ten year old daughter. I want her to receive your advance course, one-salvation. She is attending Sunday school since two yrs old and been active in music ministry, playing tambourine. But I noticed that as she grows her interests changed, I just want her to know GOD by heart and be equipped. I notice that she is interested in receiving mails, that's why I find it is a good start for her to study GODS WORD through mail, by the way, I have been saved through this ministry, back in my high school years somebody enrolled me here, and I learn more of God's word through this ministry.

The Philippines

Thank you and God Bless YOU and Your ministry.

~~~~~~

Dear Brother in Christ. I have received your Bible correspondence course. I like the course so much. And I have learned many new words about God. If it is in our Telugu Language, so many people, want to do this course. So many people can know about the word of God through this way. If you agree, I want to translate and co-ordinate your course in India. India

The Bread Of Life International
Bible Correspondence Institute

Dear Sir/Madam

I take an opportunity to read some brochure form 'THE BREAD OF LIFE' it was so thankful to in my life. I got an opportunity to learn about life, and the Bible there since I would like to learn more about life, Jesus, and Bible. Sir/Madam, If possible, please I would like to request some brochure and 1 (one) Bible below my address.

Awaiting early response.

Thanking you!
Yours faithfully
Dhaira, Dubai UAE

Dear Dr. Woodard,

I have completed the course sent to me. I am finding a possible way to send the answers to you. Our postal system is very slow and undependable. Indeed, I am blessed because your course has brought a great light and relief to most of my many doubts in the Bible. In the future, I would like to suggest if you could appoint me in Liberia to oversee some of the students that would be willing to take this worthy course. Instead of posting to them individuals, it can be posted to me, and I will distribute them and after they complete they can bring them back to me for postage. It will really be revived in my country if even 10% of our pastors in the country gone through this course.

May the Lord richly bless you and all those whom are making it possible for such a rich lessons from the Word of God to reach us in Africa.

Your student in the Lord,
Liberia

~~~~~~

Dear Dr. Johnny:

I am so glad to write after having received the course on the 9th of November. It really shows that I and my wife will benefit a lot. We will study them prayerfully and carefully so as to grow in the Faith. About the picture, I will send to you anytime.

<div align="right">
May God bless your efforts.
In Him:
Tanzania, East Africa
</div>

~~~~~~

Dr. Johnny Woodard:

Dear Sir:

I am so excited to reply you. I wasn't expecting this correspondence, it came as a surprise. I say thank you. This correspondence has really helped me. I wish the whole world had this message, there wouldn't be so much darkness.

Please always pray for me, that God would help me to preach this gospel to the end of the world.

Thanking you in anticipation to my other programs to you.

Nigeria, West Africa

CHAPTER XV

Photo Section

Jewel, Becky & Me - 1968

Me & "Ma"

Bro. Jack Walton

Me Preaching In El Gavilan, Mexico

Daddy, Me And Grandson, Michael Powers,
Shortly Before Daddy Passed Away

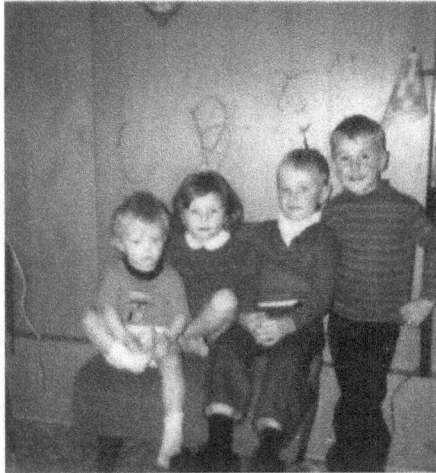

Connie, Becky, Robert & Toby Woodard

Bro. David Richmond, Bro. Ronnie Tally
and Me, Mexico - June 2008

Students With Bibles We Sent To Nigeria

Tessier Brothers With Bibles Sent To Liberia

Bro. Gary Burton & Me

Children's Class In Nepal

Bro. Billy & Sis. Page Bridges
Founders Of Bread Of Life Baptist Mission

Nepal Baptism Service

Me and Bro Paul Skinner, owner of Star Graphics Inc.,
July 2009

Me and Bro. Mackey Willis In Mexico

Australia Golf Course – 1996

Coming out of the Dome Of The Rock
Jerusalem 1995

Joe & Me with the big stringer of bass

Josh Woodard's first fish – Evans, La.

Grace Baptist Church
Mexico Mission Trip - 2008

The Woodard Family Bluegrass Gospel

Me, Connie And Becky 1976

Me, Huebert, R.L. & J.E. Woodard
July 4, 2008

The Flood Of 1953

Mama & Daddy's 50th Wedding Anniversary

Conclusion

Thank you for reading my life's story. As I look back over the years, I stand amazed at how God has worked in my life by sending special people into it. I would never have thought I would ever be able to present God's word to multitudes, as I was always a shy and timid person in school and would never stand in front of a crowd. One of the most valuable lessons one should learn from reading this book is that with God all things are possible and that He can use anyone to carry out His will.

I once heard a fellow brother in Christ say that even if there were no eternal rewards in Heaven, he would still choose to be a child of God because of the great family of God that he was associated with in his life.

I have stated many times that life is about choices, and through the years, we will face some with dire consequences. As I look back, many no doubt at times, questioned the choices I made and thought I didn't know what I was doing. What many never realize is that in order to please God, we must live by faith. While we may not understand at times what God is doing, rest assured, God always knows what is best for us and will always lead us into all truth.

My prayer is that my story will inspire you to always trust in God to lead and guide you and that you will always go forward for His great cause of reaching those who are perishing.

Some day the sun will set on our life and our work will be done. May we all be able to say that as the great Apostle Paul stated at the end of his great life of dedication to spreading God's word; *"I have finished my course, I have kept the faith."*

My favorite scripture is Luke 19:*10 "For the Son of man is come to seek and save that which was lost."* May we never get sidetracked from the path that God leads His children down, to a path that will not bring honor and glory to Him. God gave His very best, should we give less? May God inspire you to trust Him more and also rejoice in His wisdom, as we surrender our lives to His will, to be used by Him.